After-Sales Excellence

After-Sales Excellence

Driving Improvement,
Customer Satisfaction, and Growth

Nigel Woodall

BEP

BUSINESS EXPERT PRESS

Leader in applied, concise business books

After-Sales Excellence:
Driving Improvement, Customer Satisfaction, and Growth

Cover design by Harry Chiplin

Interior design by S4Carlisle Publishing Services, Chennai, India

First published in 2025 by
Business Expert Press, LLC
222 East 46th Street, New York, NY 10017
www.businessexpertpress.com

ISBN-13: 978-1-63742-888-7 (paperback)
ISBN-13: 978-1-63742-889-4 (e-book)

Sales and Salesforce Management Collection

First edition: 2025

10 9 8 7 6 5 4 3 2 1

EU SAFETY REPRESENTATIVE
Mare Nostrum Group B.V.
Mauritskade 21D
1091 GC Amsterdam
The Netherlands
gpsr@mare-nostrum.co.uk

Description

A unique book focused entirely on after-sales that is perfect for entrepreneurs, company owners, employees, students, and anyone else interested in this challenging business marketplace.

Based on the author's successful 46-year career in after-sales, as an employee, senior leader, and business management consultant, this text employs practical case studies to analyze the most commonly recurring problems that prevent the optimal performance of after-sales organizations.

Unfortunately, many times these issues either remain undetected, constantly undermining performance, or due consideration takes a backseat in the rush for solutions, often resulting in them either being far too complex or just plain wrong.

Written in a clear, concise, and logical style and leveraging the author's direct experience, the book dissects the most frequently recurring issues and presents proven solutions to them. It delivers the examples of poor practice and critical guidance for improvement in a manner that is both easily accessible and easy to understand. Essentially, it is like having your own very business consultant sat on your bookshelf for a fraction of the price.

Operating within after-sales are OEMs (Original Equipment Manufacturers) and independent stockists, distributors, repair and services organizations, replacement part manufacturers (copyists), and recyclers. They are all chasing the same customers and, in doing so, create a fast-paced, high-volume, highly complex, and constantly changing marketplace. Great customers are the "jewels" that all after-sales businesses seek, and this book will enable the reader to better understand how to address, attract, win, and keep them and ultimately deliver optimal ROI (return on investment).

Contents

List of Figures

Review Quotes

"A pragmatic and insightful, end-to-end view of the after-sales service and support marketplace. **After-Sales Excellence** *delivers a concise and practical roadmap to both overcome and proactively avoid the common challenges that prevent success."*—**Toby Chisnall, Ridgeline Consulting**

Acknowledgments

I want to thank those who have supported me in this book-writing endeavor. In particular, I would like to extend thanks to my two brothers, Dave and Andy, as well as Bjorn, Toby Chisnall, Glyn "old pal" Henderson, Steve Poole, Kevin Yaremchuk, and Kevin Michaels of AeroDynamic Advisory, for their help with proofreading, review, and, of course, reminders on the points I had forgotten.

I would also like to extend my sincere thanks to my ex-colleagues, peers, and mentors whose experience and support (always freely given) have undoubtedly shaped my career. I also can't forget my many customers. We've shared some great times, and it has been a very enjoyable journey (admittedly sometimes less so—you know who you are!), but it was never less than challenging and thought-provoking.

I wanted to make the book a "local" project, and so a special mention and thanks goes to Harry Chiplin, for the fantastic cover design. Harry is an ex-Brockenhurst College student who is also undertaking a graphic design degree at Solent University.

Finally, a well-earned mention to my family, who have supported and encouraged me throughout.

To all the above—you have helped me enjoy both a successful career and reach this point today. Here's a heartfelt thank you to all—please take a bow!

Preface

Throughout my 46-year career, the B2B (Business to Business) after-sales (aka aftermarket) arena has been the focus. Since midcareer, I have been fortunate enough to have had senior leadership roles with original equipment manufacturers (OEMs) and independent maintenance, repair, and overhaul (MRO) and distribution organizations. These roles have been in the customer-facing areas of after-sales, including, customer service, account management, field service, technical support, reliability, warranty, sales, marketing, contracts, and commercial. That time served has provided me with an unusually broad and deep understanding of the marketplace.

The COVID-19 pandemic lockdown provided time to reflect on what I had achieved in my career. This period of personal reflection was crucial as it defined my genuine enjoyment of roles that were an enabler to driving positive transformation within organizations, as well as mentoring and fostering the growth of others. Having always been an employee to that point, I decided it was time for a change, and so, since 2021, I have been running my own after-sales consultancy practice.

The idea for this book grew out of conversations with colleagues and clients, as we all agreed that the after-sales sector is underserved when it comes to dedicated written resources. With me approaching the latter part of my business life, they were also concerned about the potential loss of my accumulated knowledge—prompting their encouragement to document and share the key insights I have gathered over the course of career. Those discussions, together with the ongoing demand for my consulting services, convinced me as to the relevance of my expertise for individuals and SMEs and, therefore, I took the plunge.

Many business books are heavyweight deep-dives with a strong theoretical focus, which can make them challenging for business practitioners, and other interested readers to relate to. In contrast, this book is grounded entirely in my direct and indirect real world experience, focusing only on the most common issues that routinely affect after-sales business performance. My aim has been to create something both practical and enlightening. It offers a wealth of examples and proven solutions to the recurring problems that hold businesses back and lead to suboptimal results.

The presentation is deliberately generic, as the market sector where I gained my experience may differ from your own. However, the basic principles and challenges of sales support—whether after-sales or OEM—such as managing customer, supplier, and competitor relationships, are similar in all businesses. Hence, what I am presenting will fall somewhere in the middle of being partially and fully transferrable. Nevertheless, I recommend that all business types can benefit from broadening their perspectives by exploring ideas and best practices from outside their immediate industry and market.

Ultimately, my goal is to create a valuable, reusable resource for anyone interested in the after-sales marketplace, including entrepreneurs, businesses, individual practitioners, investors, and students.

Finally, I have tried to avoid writing this in the typical dry style of many business textbooks. Hopefully, this and the other elements referred to above combine successfully to make it an accessible, enjoyable, and, most importantly, valuable read.

This book includes instructor materials. Please contact charlene .kronstedt@businessexpertpress.com to request the accompanying ancillaries.

Glossary of Terms

Like any marketplace, the after-sales market uses a wide range of acronyms and terms that will vary across businesses and sectors.

This book uses definitions adjusted to its content; expect minor deviations from standard practice.

%BOM: Proportional Bill of Material.

A %BOM comprises a structured list of all the materials, parts, components, assemblies, subassemblies, and other items required to repair, service, or overhaul a product. Each item within the complete product to be repaired has an individually assigned percentage representing its likelihood of being required during a single repair.

For example, 10 percent would mean that one in every ten repairs would require the item.

Aftermarket:

The term "aftermarket" is commonly used to refer to after-sales, making the two terms fully interchangeable. See After-sales.

After-sales:

After-sales (aka Aftermarket) is the market for replacement parts (spares), accessories, equipment, and value-added services for the care (maintenance, repair, and overhaul) or enhancement of the original product. One example of the many types of after-sales products and services includes the ongoing maintenance (spare parts and labor) of an automobile, after its sale to the consumer. Further examples include replacement printer ink cartridges, lawnmower repairs, and the ongoing servicing of machinery in a food processing plant.

AI: Artificial Intelligence.

AI refers to technology that allows computers to perform tasks that normally require human minds.

APD: After-sales Price Differential.

Some organizations price their initial OEM production sale of a new product as either a loss-maker or at a significantly reduced margin. An APD is the price gap between OEM production sales and after-sales marketplace sales of an identical item. In such business models, after-sales typically become the mechanism through which the OEMs rebalance their overall financial model.

BAFO: Best and Final Offer.

A BAFO represents a supplier offer made to a customer during commercial negotiations. Within a bid scenario, the BAFO will contain the absolute best terms the supplier can offer, from the customer's perspective. Any demand to exceed these terms should require a complete internal financial review and re-approval before submission to a customer. BAFO and going in (GI) positions should be defined and approved in parallel (see also "GI").

Business Process Reengineering:

Business process reengineering is the radical redesign of business processes to achieve dramatic improvements in the following: efficiency, effectiveness, performance and cycle times, quality, costs, and both employee and customer satisfaction.

CBRM: Customer Business Review Meeting:

A meeting between supplier and customer—typically where a customer is of strategic or high sales value. The meetings usually operate on a mutually agreed agenda and will include the overall health of the relationship and a review of agreed Key Performance Indicators (KPIs).

Concurrent Design:

Concurrent design employs a multidisciplined team approach. This approach combines the theoretical knowledge of the OEM team with the direct knowledge about existing product performance and customer usage from the after-sales team. Reflecting this combined knowledge within the new designs delivers long-term benefits. For example, first-time design success minimizes the requirement for subsequent product redesign and potential associated warranty costs.

Cost of Ownership:

The cost of ownership encompasses the overall cost incurred to operate a product or service throughout its full life, including both the direct and indirect costs. For example, for a petrol lawnmower, this would include the initial purchase price, plus servicing costs (oil, grease, etc.), any projected scheduled/unscheduled repair, and the cost of fuel. The use of the term "lifecycle costs" is interchangeable with "cost of ownership."

CRM: Customer Relationship Management.

A centralized technology-based system for the management of processes, communications, and relationships with customers.

C-Sat: Customer Satisfaction.

A measure of a customer's satisfaction with an organization's products, services, and/or interactions.

Delegated Authority:

The action of entrusting and allowing another individual to be approved to make decisions on your behalf.

DXP: Digital Experience Platform.

A software platform that will help companies create, manage, deliver, and optimize digital experiences across multiple channels. DXPs can be a single product or a suite of products that work together. They can help companies digitize their operations, become more efficient, provide better customer experiences, and gather customer insights.

EIS: Entry into Service.

Entry into Service is the point at which a new product or service ceases its internal development phase and enters active general usage with the target market.

ERP: Enterprise Resource Planning.

ERP refers to a type of business management software that organizations use to manage day-to-day core business activities optimally. It is typically a suite of integrated applications that an organization can use to collect, store, manage, and interpret data from its many core activities. ERP manages the flow of data between a company's business processes, providing a single source of truth and streamlining operations across the organization.

Generative AI:

Is a type of AI that can produce new content. Generative AI models learn patterns and structures of data that enable them to create new data with similar characteristics.

GI: Going In.

"Going In" defines a supplier's initial approved bid within customer negotiations. The GI serves as the supplier's most advantageous bidding level when launching their bid with the customer. GI and BAFO positions should be defined and approved in parallel. See also "BAFO."

GTA: General Terms Agreement.

A GTA distils the repetitive standard terms and conditions that feature in individual supply and service agreements into a single umbrella agreement. Subsequent supply and service agreements can be slotted under and subject to the GTA terms and conditions. Having such an agreement in place removes the necessity of repeating standard terms and conditions in every single agreement. Consequently, negotiating future supply and service agreements with a client will be easier and quicker.

Hidden Factory:

These are any actions and activities that include "bug," "process," and "product" workarounds that routinely occur outside of any formal instruction or recording method. Individuals within a process usually carry out these actions and activities, passing them down from employee to employee through word-of-mouth or informal written instructions. For example, a critical assembly component, though meeting specifications, might need manual adjustment. The activities of the Hidden Factory can be crucial to a business meeting its production and/or delivery targets.

Infant Mortality:

>Failures of product or service that occur prematurely. Such failures can occur because of the following: customer's incorrect design specification, poor or insufficient design, inadequate testing, inferior material, and poor workmanship.

IP:

>Intellectual Property.
>
>Typically, people define IP as any type of invention, design, logo, symbol, image, trademark, name, or anything that someone writes, makes, or produces.

JIT:

>Just in Time.
>
>JIT is an operational strategy that aims to align product/material orders from suppliers directly with production schedules. Organizations deploy this inventory management strategy to increase efficiency and decrease waste by receiving goods only as and when they need them within their production process. This strategy can offer significant financial benefits over "just in case" inventory management but requires organizations to forecast their demand accurately.

Key Account Management:

>Is a strategy where an organization provides the personnel and resources to create a mutually beneficial partnership between itself and its most valuable and/or important customers. Key accounts are significant to an organization's sustainable, long-term growth and require a significant investment of both labor and resources.

KPI:

>Key Performance Indicator.
>
>KPIs are a quantifiable measurement of performance and success (or lack thereof) over time in relation to a specific target. In many companies, KPIs for each department are part of a structure that creates a balanced scorecard to ensure relevance and alignment with the overall business strategy.

LLM:

>Large Language Model.
>
>A type of AI program trained on large collections of text data that will enable it to recognize, interpret, and generate human-like language. LLMs are used for generative AI to

produce human-like language responses to input prompts, for example, in chatbots and virtual assistants.

Master data:

Master data are the core data critical to the running of a business enterprise or unit. These data are the unique information that describes core entities for a business and includes product, supplier, and customer information. It ensures that accurate and consistent data are managed and available across the operating systems of a business, such as ERP and CRM. It removes the improper formatting roadblocks and base data errors that impede data sharing and analysis in an organization. Therefore, it is commonly called a "golden record" of information or the "best source of truth." Examples of master data include a customer's business name, address, and telephone number, as well as a product's part number, description, and the platform it is used within.

MRO: Maintenance, Repair, and Overhaul.

Refers to the action of returning an unserviceable (faulty) product to a fully serviceable/working condition.

NLP: Natural Language Processing.

NLP is an area of AI that allows computers to understand, create, and manipulate human language. Essentially, it allows a computer to both listen and speak in a human-like manner.

NPS: Net Promoter Score.

A metric used in customer satisfaction programs. NPS measures the loyalty of customers to a business by using a quick survey (usually one question).

OEM: Original Equipment Manufacturer.

Refers to the original approved manufacturer of the part or product.

OOP: Out of Production.

Means that an OEM's production (manufacturing) run has ended and, therefore, any ongoing manufacturing and support is to meet after-sales demand only. For example, while Ford stopped their production run for their Fiesta in 2023, the car will remain in service for many years to come. Consequently, spare parts will remain in constant demand.

ORT: Opportunity Review Team.

The team responsible for ensuring that only those sales opportunities that meet an organization's minimum requirements proceed.

ORT meetings provide the initial review and approval to proceed with an opportunity. Subsequently, they provide the intermediate and final approvals prior to proposals being issued to a customer.

ORT meetings can either be ad hoc or scheduled and typically comprise a defined group of senior stakeholders, including authorized decision-makers, such as those in finance, operations, and so on. The meetings can vary widely in length depending on deal importance/complexity and so on.

PMA: Parts Manufacturer Approval.

An aerospace industry approval to allow an organization to design, manufacture, and sell alternative parts to those available from the OEM.

Product: A *product* can mean a spare part, or a complete assembly, or oil, greases, and so on. Any reference to *product* can also equally mean service as appropriate.

RFP: Request for Proposal.

An RFP is a document that usually announces a project and contains all the detailed specifications and terms that relate to the project. An RFP invites suppliers to bid on customer projects, often involving complex bids and long-term sales.

RFQ: Request for Quotation.

An RFQ is a document within which a customer company invites a supplier to submit a price quote for a product or service. RFQs typically relate to the day-to-day transactional, one-off sales.

RMU: Retrofit, Modification, and Upgrade.

A series of actions that can replace, change/improve, and/or add benefits to a product. Such actions can provide opportunities for increased revenue, reduced cost, and improved customer satisfaction.

S&OP: Sales and Operations Planning.

An integrated management process driving both alignment and synchronization of purpose across critical functions, thereby ensuring the business is enabled to meet its strategic delivery aims.

SA%:   Schedule Adherence.

The measure of the delivery performance of a business, that is, how much of their product they deliver early/on time versus deliver late. It is usually presented as a percentage score.

Servitization:

The concept of servitization in the after-sales marketplace relates to the transformation from a product-centric focus to a service-oriented business model. Such services can enhance existing value propositions or to add new opportunities for chargeable activities.

Six Sigma: Six Sigma is a methodology that provides an organization with the tools to improve the efficiency and effectiveness of their processes. It applies statistics, financial analysis, and project management to both identify and correct mistakes or defects in existing processes. The improved performance and decreased process variation help drive defect reduction and improvement in profits, employee morale, and quality of products or services. There are five phases to the Six Sigma method, known as DMAIC (defining, measuring, analyzing, improving, and controlling).

Smart Scoping:

Refers to reduction of labor and material usage during the MRO process via the application of product-focused technical evaluations.

SME: Small- and Medium-Sized Enterprise.

According to the UK government, an SME is any organization that has fewer than 250 employees and a turnover of less than €50 million or a balance sheet total less than €43 million.

Spares: The term "spares" denotes both individual components and complete assemblies. For instance, you can classify the sale of a starter motor for your car as a "spare." You can also classify each of the individual parts that make up that same starter motor as "spares," for example, nuts, bolts, washers, springs, and so on.

STTE: Special Tools and Test Equipment.
             Refers to any non-general tooling and test equipment that is product specific. STTE is typically identified within the technical publications that support a product, for example, component maintenance manuals, and repair and/or servicing manuals.

Sunset: During the sunset phase, businesses typically view a product or service as being less economically and/or strategically viable. Therefore, firms will either discontinue or outsource this product/service.

TAT: Turnaround Time.
             TAT refers to the time taken by a supplier to repair a product. Measurement typically runs from customer receipt to return shipment.

USM: Used Serviceable Material.
             Refers to parts that have been previously used in service and which are subsequently stored in a serviceable (usable) condition.

USP: Unique Selling Point.
             Also referred to as a unique selling proposition. It is the essence of what makes your product or service better than your competitors and is therefore a critical point of differentiation. It can comprise a single point or multiple points.

Value Proposition:
             A value proposition identifies the true benefits/value that a business states it will deliver to a customer of its products and/or services. The business should construct the inherent value from the customer's perspective and not against internal business measures.
             A value proposition must distinguish a business from competitors, clearly explaining customer purchase rationale.

A business can apply a value proposition to its entire operation, a specific function within the business, or a particular product/service.

VOC: Voice of the Customer.

The formal process that directly solicits customer feedback about their experiences with and expectations for the products and/or services that a business provides.

CHAPTER 1

Introduction

After-sales is a vast global marketplace. It includes everything from replacement light bulbs and maintenance (repair and Spare parts) and post-sales support for white goods such as washing machines, to equipment for industries like farming, oil, gas, aerospace, and nuclear (and more).

To provide context to the size and importance of this market segment, here are the 2025 forecasts for just three examples (two business to business [B2B] and one business to consumer [B2C]).

- Global light duty automotive (essentially cars and small vans) will reach $444B (Statista 2023).
- The commercial air transport (civil passenger and cargo aircraft) *maintenance, repair, and overhaul (MRO)* will be worth over $100B (Oliver Wyman 2023).
- The coffee capsule market will exceed $16B (The Business Research Company 2024).

There are many more sectors that form part of the total global after-sales marketplace—which is estimated to generate over ***$9 trillion annually*** (figure extrapolated from Aberdeen Group estimate of US aftermarket size (cited Cohen et al. 2006, 1) and World Bank Group global and US GDP data (World Bank Group, 2025).

The after-sales marketplace is also a cornerstone of sustainability, extending product lifespans, reducing waste, conserving resources, cutting emissions, supporting the circular economy, and promoting responsible consumption. Through timely repairs, maintenance, and upgrades, it prevents premature disposal, while refurbishment and component replacement keep products in use for years rather than months. This, in turn, reduces the demand for new manufacturing—the largest contributor to many products' environmental footprints. Beyond protecting the environment, after-sales services enhance the economic and practical value of products for businesses and customers alike. Given its scale, environmental impact, and integration into the daily lives of organisations, investors, consumers, and communities, the sector's performance and reliability are vital to us all.

At its most basic level, what is it that an after-sales customer wants from its suppliers? They want suppliers to provide justifiably priced, reliable *products*, services, and support that perform as advertised. They expect these to be delivered within acceptable lead times, consistently on time, and accompanied by responsive, helpful communication. In summary, the customer desires satisfaction encompassing the purchasing decision, sales experience, and post-purchase support.

If your business has been meeting customer expectations and performing consistently well, then it is time to cheer for yourselves. However, I would also suggest that you continue to read on, as I have yet to find a business that is anywhere near perfect.

In reality, delivering a product to meet customers' immediate needs is only a qualifier—it is a transactional approach.

Some organizations may prioritize immediate profitability; however, a truly sustainable and successful after-sales organization is built upon customer loyalty and repeat business. As Chip Bell, customer loyalty guru and author said, "Customers who are merely satisfied will remain your customers only as long as everything goes their way" (Bell and Patterson 2007, xx). This clearly reveals the ever-present danger in "just doing enough."

What sets successful businesses apart is their capacity to foster loyalty by surpassing customer expectations through outstanding performance and added value. This higher service level provides more than customers thought they wanted and more than they thought they needed. This is integral to the art of building a sustainable competitive advantage (Heppell 2015, 14–15).

Delivering performance is an operational challenge, whereas adding value is a conceptual challenge (initially), requiring a business to think differently and switch from a transactional focus to a services strategy. We call this *servitization*, and this book provides many examples. Remember, this activity will happen in a competitive setting and, therefore, the business demands will be constantly moving.

Alternatively, what is it the after-sales organizations themselves want? Well, from my experience, it is simply to deliver products and services to customers at the highest price and lowest cost. They will typically want to have an acceptable level of customer service, while growing the business year over year (preferably higher than organic market growth). Finally, they want to be respected by their customers.

These requirements combine to present the supplier/customer business equation that needs to be solved. Furthermore, as the marketplaces in which we operate are constantly evolving, it would make sense that how we answer today's challenge will differ from how it needs to be answered tomorrow. Instead, our response is something that constantly needs to be addressed and rebalanced. Therefore, to achieve after-sales excellence, businesses must constantly adapt to evolving marketplace demands, balancing the needs of customers, plus responding to the actions of suppliers and competitors.

It is also worth considering some rather sobering data that states for the 10 years up to and including 2023, within two years, 20 percent of the private sector business startups in 2013 had failed. By Year 5, that figure has risen to approximately 50 percent and by Year 10, only approximately 35 percent remained in operation (U.S. Bureau of Labor Statistics 2024). I could not find a data source for the UK, but general commentary appears to point to similar results. Furthermore, the results of a postmortem analysis of 101 failed startups (CB Insights cited Fortune 2014) showed the 20 most given reasons for business failure were self-inflicted wounds of one sort or another—for example, poor planning and strategy deployment, inconsistent execution and mistaken decision-making, and so on. The financial statistics associated with poor customer service are equally eye-opening. The UK Institute of Customer Service states the cost of poor service is an astonishing £7.3B per month within the UK (The Institute of Customer Service 2025). The Qualtrics XM Institute estimated that globally, as customers reduce their spending with poor service providers, $3.7 trillion of sales were at risk from bad experiences in 2024 (QualtricsXM 2024). These astronomical figures highlight not only the negative effects of poor service but also the potential benefits to be gained from improvement. While none of these examples has a specific after-sales focus, being drawn from various market sectors, they offer a cross-sectional perspective and remain directionally pertinent.

I want to clarify that I am not implying that mismanagement or human error are the sole cause of all failed businesses. There are many external factors, such as war, pandemic, regulation, and social changes, which can also contribute to their downfall. Nevertheless, a significant number of businesses have either failed or compromised their performance because of poor decision-making.

Some may also ask "Why write a book on after-sales, surely the core issues are potentially present in any business?" and I acknowledge there is validity in this point. But, as my clients have pointed out many times, there are few books available aimed purely at after-sales. So, this text takes a different approach, choosing to focus only on those repetitive issues within an after-sales context. That said, it is also fair to say that many of the themes raised will also have applicability to a much broader marketplace.

In summary, after-sales is a very competitive and complex marketplace. Many *original equipment manufacturers (OEMs)*, independent stockists, distributors, repair services, copycat part-makers, and recyclers are chasing the same customers. The required velocity, high transaction volume, and significant customer base amplify the negative effects of poor post-purchase service.

Given the challenging, dynamic market, high customer expectations, and the history of underperformance, I believe this book is necessary. In the pages that follow, you will find both examples of and proven solutions to some of the most common issues that cause that underperformance and prevent after-sales businesses (and many others) from achieving their true potential.

CHAPTER 2

The Business Challenge

There is only one boss. The customer. And he can fire everybody in the company from the chairman on down, simply by spending his money somewhere else.

—Sam Walton, founder of Walmart and Sam's Club.

Any business can offer an array of products and services and make many promises about them, but if they cannot deliver them professionally, consistently, or at all, they are meaningless. I have seen many organizations seeking competitive advantage that elect to follow the all-encompassing service approach, while still delivering mediocre performance on the basics. Unsurprisingly, without a true focus on their performance and the customer, everything follows the same path of mediocrity.

In fact, service excellence is not about the breadth and depth of the services and products that a business offers. Instead, the critical factor is their performance in delivering those services and products—how they meet their promises and commitments. Consequently, service excellence is about the performance of the fundamental delivery mechanisms—their quality and sustainability.

Fundamentally, core performance should not offer competitive advantage; sadly, however, poor execution plagues many businesses. Therefore, excellent service can act as the key differentiator between otherwise similar competitors in a way that is truly meaningful to customers (Zeithaml et al. 1990, 10).

Throughout my business career, I have been a customer of, worked with, for and alongside, and also a supplier to and competed with (and sometimes all at the same time) many different organizations. Those interactions, along with the fact that I have spent my working life in B2B after-sales services, have allowed me to refine my ability to identify both good and bad customer service.

To be fair, all the successful businesses I have encountered have a common theme—a strong focus on their customers. But today's after-sales marketplace has evolved significantly in terms of its needs and desires compared to when I first started.

With the emergence of social media and the demand for immediate satisfaction, customer expectations are now increasing at a faster rate than ever before. Some may argue that most of these developments occur in the consumer space (B2C). However, these trends are also rolling through B2B, and why would they not, as it is all about customers—made up of people? The challenge for many businesses is that workplace technology and management practice have not caught up yet—leading to a customer satisfaction gap.

It is also entirely possible for a business to be "successful" and still never actually achieve its full potential. Over the years, I have worked with many organizations that believed they were performing well, but, upon closer inspection, multiple shortcomings were apparent. The question within those organizations effectively became "*if we can resolve the issues, just how much better can we be?*" Traditionally, organizations that are content with their achievements become complacent and then adopt an "if it's not broken, don't fix it" mentality, a position that is frequently not supported by any data or reality.

No market stands still—customers' needs and expectations are constantly changing. Competitors constantly attack a business's most attractive aspects. Businesses often cannot grasp supplier performance and strategy, while technology constantly advances.

Ricardo Semler, CEO of Semco Partners and proponent of employee-friendly radical industrial democracy, highlighted the mismatch between rapid technological advancements and our slow-changing mindsets. He used the example of a woolen mill's hierarchical structure in 1633 and the fact the same overbearing, top-down management, with close and distrustful supervision, still exists in many businesses today (Semler 1999, 269). This is a great example of how many companies have not changed with the times, failing to update and adopt modern approaches to business management.

Based on my career observations, here are the common challenges facing after-sales businesses, some of which you may relate to.

The After-Sales Conundrum

My experience with different original equipment manufacturers (OEMs) has been that delivering high-quality after-sales support has been a continual struggle. It rarely seems like customer centricity is a priority for these organizations.

Some companies focus heavily on the original production equipment, neglect after-sales, and treat it as an afterthought, creating a significant disparity between them. The *Harvard Business Review* also confirmed this position, writing "Most companies either don't know how or don't care to provide after-sales services effectively. Top managements the world over treat Aftermarket services as a mere afterthought" (Cohen et al. 2006, 1).

This has always surprised me, considering the much greater complexity of this market sector. Frequently, it must support all the OEMs past, present, and new products, along with their respective customers. The production (design, manufacturing, etc.) side of an OEM may be restricted to just one or two sites. However, the after-sales division may extend across various national and international locations, each requiring overseeing personnel, machinery, and supplies.

Maybe this "after-sales oversight" occurs because CEOs often come from OEM or finance environments. Executives from these backgrounds may struggle to adapt to customer-centric markets with less predictable demands. While this may be contributory, I feel this is a location issue as much as anything else; CEOs base themselves either in a head office, or within the OEM facilities, as opposed to the after-sales division. I believe that this proximity to all things OEM is the prime driver behind the after-sales blind spot.

There can also be a prevailing view that customer service is not a value addition because of the difficulty in quantifying its ROI. This might seem quite bizarre, given an OEM may need to obtain a significant portion of their turnover and overall profit margin from after-sales to make their business models work.

They achieve this through two means, the first of which is the longevity of the products. Long lifecycles provide the opportunity for significant ongoing revenue to be earned from services, *spares*, MRO, and support activity. For example, the average lifecycle of a commercial jet aircraft was

22.8 years in 2019 (Statista 2024) and the average life of a car in the UK was 17 years at the end of 2023 (CarTakeBack 2023).

The second method is something I refer to as the *after-sales price differential (APD)*. Essentially, this is the difference in price charged for the product on its original sale by the OEM and the subsequent price of those same products when sold via its after-sales division. This allows for a higher financial return. Deloitte referred to this variance as follows: "Today, the average operating margin from an after-sales business globally is about two point five times the operating margin from new equipment sales" (Deloitte 2020).

If you are not an OEM but are instead operating as an independent business, then you will already understand just how important after-sales are to you. Independent suppliers have an ingrained need to perform, and, based on my observations, they consistently do a better job than the OEM after-sales services. That said, there are still significant challenges, not least with their own management issues, reliance on OEM supply chains, and questions around their relationship with them (true independence, partner or hybrid). Finally, the competitive element is no less complex for an independent versus an OEM supplier.

Market Segmentation

Whether you are a brand new business in the making, or an established business, the following advice applies equally. It is crucial to strike a balance between the desired customer base for your business and the practicality of your organization's capabilities and resources. For example, you might decide that you want to target those customers who focus on the ticket price above all else. Of course, such a narrow approach to the customer base will make for a less complex business, but it will also immediately disenfranchise those customers who desire a more encompassing, feature-laden service. Consequently, the market you can target will be a subset of the total market size available, which raises its own questions about the existing competitive landscape and indeed whether it can support your business as well.

Alternatively, you may wish to go to the complete opposite end of the spectrum and offer a very broad range of service options that permit an array of bespoke tailoring to meet individual customer needs. This certainly allows for higher pricing and the widest possible marketplace for your business to operate within. Of course, while having such high service flexibility can be a great aim, there is also no question that it brings with it significantly higher complexity, effort, and cost for any supplier to manage.

For a business to operate in this way means it is very performance dependent. That may seem obvious to say, but if you try to operate in the full-service guise, never lose sight of the impact that service excellence has on your customer base. Essentially, if you cannot deliver what you promise, your business will quickly find itself competing only with those much simpler businesses in the price-focused segment of the market, despite having significantly higher prices and costs.

The Service Challenge

Wilson et al. (2012, 51) refer to the fact that having both a thorough knowledge and clear understanding of customer expectations is possibly the most critical step in delivering good quality service.

According to a survey of 1,000 customers, the primary reason for them to give a positive recommendation was a business consistently fulfilling its promises (Heppell 2015, 44). Therefore, knowing what a customer wants is one challenge, but the next most important hurdle is to identify whether a business can deliver it. Therein lays the risk, as research shows that for every individual complaint a company receives, there are about 20 to 100 other customers who experienced the same issue but did not complain (Wilson et al. 2012, 51).

The implications for reputational damage caused by negative service should not be a surprise to anyone reading this book. Just take a moment to consider your own buying behaviors. How many of you have decided to never use a supplier again because of a poor service (and passed on details of the negative experience to friends, family, and colleagues)?

Unfortunately, suppliers often fail to recognize the significant business costs associated with unmet customer commitments. These will include the resources required to deliver a resolution and potentially being barred from future bids, or customers simply directing their business elsewhere. In addition, other financial costs could include contractual service penalties.

Business Philosophy

Unfortunately, in many organizations, the senior management's view of the customer-facing team within after-sales has been less than positive—"They are a cost of doing business." This perspective stems from the belief that staff who do not directly add value to the product (unlike shopfloor staff) do not contribute to the success of the business to the same extent.

It is usually a supplier's customer-facing personnel who are vocalizing and pressuring colleagues about poor performance, and this is entirely natural given their proximity to and familiarity with the customers. To be honest, if they were not acting in this way, I would be concerned because they are simply acting in the customers' best interests within the organization. However, it can build internal animosity, and you may frequently hear comments like "oh, they've defected to the other side." Ultimately, this type of negative response shows that not all individuals within the organization prioritize customer satisfaction in the same way.

I have found this line of thinking is completely misguided. Allowing it to continue unchallenged will weaken after-sales organizations and hinder their ability to maximize financial returns for the business.

Short-termism

Short-termism in after-sales is self-defeating as the sector is all about repeat sales and the ongoing support/maintenance of products and services through their lifecycle. According to research, companies with the highest customer loyalty scores in their industries grow revenue two point five times faster than their industry peers and secure two to five times the shareholder returns over 10 years (Markey 2020, 4). On that basis, a longer-term strategy should always be the way forward.

Perhaps surprisingly, there have only been a few occasions during my career when I have experienced the "sweet spot" of after-sales support being reached (see Technical Support). Happy customers, solid sales growth, job satisfaction, and team spirit made for a fabulous working environment. Unfortunately, most of the times it proved to be transient, as subsequent corporate earnings pressure drove short-term decision-making.

An example of the former was an organization with a long-term reputation for its unreliable MRO delivery performance. The primary issue was the unreliable supply of parts from the OEM to its own after-sales division, which, despite repeated efforts over a significant timeframe, could not resolve their manufacturing challenges. This resulted in their failure to support improved delivery.

Finally, recognizing that a resolution would likely never appear, the after-sales business started investing in *used serviceable material (USM)* to create an "exchange pool." This pool was to provide an inventory buffer to allow the business to complete exchanges for any item of customer equipment delayed within the MRO process. Effectively, whenever parts shortages caused a delay that would impact MRO performance, the customer would be offered a like-for-like exchange from the pool; that is, it would have a similar service life expired and an equal warranty. If the customer approved the exchange, the title (ownership) of their equipment within the process would transfer to the MRO business. As their part of the exchange, the MRO business would transfer the title of an item from its pool to the customer and thereby complete the order within the originally required delivery window.

The after-sales team gradually built up a large inventory pool and, as a direct result, achieved significant improvements in their delivery performance. However, the OEM parent used a variety of strategies to hit their financial targets, and these included inventory "fire sales" at quarter and year end. It was during just one such period, when the OEM, searching for "gap fill" sales, spotted the pool stock held by after-sales and ordered its immediate sale. Despite protestations and explanations about the damaging effects on service levels, after-sales had no choice but to comply.

Unsurprisingly, losing the exchange pool with no fix for the OEM delivery issues left the business exposed. Performance reverted to the previously poor position, together with a resultant negative impact on their revenue.

The Growth Challenge

Most organizations want to achieve year-on-year growth, and their own-ers, boards, and investors often expect them to achieve higher rates than what the market naturally offers. However, unless those organizations are introducing new products and services, or diversifying into other mar-kets, then it can only come from one other area—their competitors. By default, those competitors will already be suppliers to the existing cus-tomer base, and so the challenge of how to take market share begins.

But just because you want growth, that does not mean it will come to you automatically. You must earn it, and doing the same things you have always done will just produce the same results. Therefore, to meet growth requirements in such circumstances, your business is going to have to do something different to create a new *value proposition* for the customers.

Leaky Bucket Syndrome

Sometimes, even if you grow your sales with new customers, the "leaky bucket syndrome" can nullify the overall effects. This is where existing customers are walking away completely or spending less because they have found a better/more reliable supplier.

Replacing lost customers is bad for business, and here is why: The *Harvard Business Review* shows acquiring new customers costs 5 to 25 times more than keeping existing ones. They also say that increasing customer retention rates by 5 percent increases profits by between 25 and 95 percent (Gallo 2014, 1).

My observations support these statistics, and I would also say that many breakthrough ideas (new projects and sales opportunities) have al-ways been a direct consequence of the strong relationships with existing customers. It is simply that existing clients are more willing to invest time in working with their selected suppliers. This has been especially import-ant when it comes to "blue sky" development projects.

Given the above, I cannot stress the importance of retaining existing customers highly enough, and, therefore, it is not enough to solely focus on finding new customers; you must also prioritize keeping and growing your existing customer base.

It is also interesting to note that businesses with a track record of good service can keep customers even during periods of poor performance. This can provide them with the opportunity to address issues without significant damage to sales. It involves cultivating "sticky customers," who remain loyal even during challenging times.

How do customers become "sticky"? One reason is they recognize that a business shows through its performance and behaviors that it "has their back" in those critical moments and it is always striving to do the right thing.

Rebranding and Reorganization

At the macro level, organizations have made very extensive investment in completely rebranding their businesses. They do this to "jettison" their association with their (poor) past or to become more "relevant" to their customers.

I have also seen businesses swallowing the "we need a new management system" pill. This has resulted in the deployment of highly complex, time-consuming, overarching business management systems to improve their performance. However, most of the times, these activities have been quite internal, with a focus and output that did not prioritize the customer as much as expected.

Failing to understand customer needs and expectations hinders the ability to establish the appropriate organizational structure and capabilities to meet those needs. Thus, the potential for a strengthened business partnership and positive results is compromised.

Competition

If it is not enough to cope with the above elements, along come the competitive vultures circling your business. So, not only must you manage your customers' needs and expectations, but you must also keep a wary eye on your competitors.

In too many businesses, there can be a very negative and/or derogatory view of competitors, but I do not believe this is healthy. First, it is always worth remembering that your own business is also a competitor of your competitors and, consequently, would happily take their customers and market share if the opportunity arose. Second, if the competitors are being successful in taking your customers, they must be doing something right and you must be doing something wrong (or less well). The correct mindset would therefore be to take a step back and analyze just how they are eating your lunch.

My belief has always been that businesses should embrace competition, as it prevents them from getting too comfortable. Instead, it drives constant innovation—it forces suppliers to think differently, and competitive market developments can also open the eyes of a business to new opportunities.

Renowned author and thought leader in business and competition strategy, Michael E. Porter, says that competitors can be a threat to a business, but the right competitors can strengthen rather than weaken their competitive advantage—for example, lowering the threat of legal challenges for anticompetitive behavior from a market-dominant position or serving unattractive segments and customers (Porter 2004, 202–212). Many times, I have proactively worked with competitors to extract mutual benefit from situations where there had only previously been discord and negativity.

In summary, competition is an enduring fact of life that will never disappear. Therefore, it is preferable to adopt a positive approach and develop a strategy to professionally manage it, rather than react negatively and harbor resentment.

Superhuman Versus Super Service

Having worked with organizations with both good and bad performance, I would simply say that a well-run after-sales business will be a singularly more pleasant and smooth-running workplace. Sure, you can have your own version of a superhuman flitting around your business putting out the "fires" as they spring up. But each of those challenges and the subsequent "get well" activity will have a draining effect on both resources and your staff generally.

The significance of that customer pressure should not be understated, given that frontline staff continually strive to resolve issues, address complaints, and manage irate clients. Neglecting this matter will ultimately cultivate a negative atmosphere, undesirable behaviors, and difficulties with employee retention.

Finally, it is worth emphasizing that only the very best and most successful organizations know how to understand, maximize, and, most importantly, deliver their full potential consistently.

CHAPTER 3

Information Management and Planning

Enterprise Resource Planning Systems

It may seem an obvious thing to say, but your business will only ever be as good as the processes and systems that are running within it. Therefore, having an appropriate *enterprise resource planning (ERP)* system supporting your business would seem like a straightforward decision.

Improved efficiency, data management, scalability, operating costs, and inventory management are just a few of the potential benefits. Unsurprisingly, if you asked any CEO, he would tell you it is a necessary and critical part of business.

Conversely, without the right tools to do the job, even the best and the most highly trained staff will struggle. This can lead to poor or, at best, suboptimal performance, including a negative impact on sales and margin. So, while many businesses ensure their ERP is a correct fit, we do also need to ask just why so many organizations get this wrong.

It is worth pausing to understand that an OEM's design/manufacturing and after-sales are very different propositions, with the latter being considerably more complex. Here are just some examples of why my experience shows the after-sales environment needs to have an ERP specifically aligned to their needs:

- **Products and Services**
  The additional services provided can present significant challenges, for example, the management of product exchange and loans and the financial accounting for usage-based billing.

  Moreover, if there has been no significant divestment or a clear *sunset* strategy implemented, the after-sales business will probably need to support all the OEM's past, current, and future product lines.

- **Customers**
In almost all cases, the customer base of an OEM will be significantly smaller than that of its after-sales division.
- **Locations**
OEMs will probably have one or two manufacturing hubs. The after-sales structure for that same business could have multiple national and internationally based service sites, all of which require the management of facilities, equipment, people, and products/parts.
- **Tempo**
After-sales operates to a different drumbeat than an OEM, as the latter generally have long lead times built into their DNA, whether that is product inception, design, manufacturing, or delivery. OEMs talk about delivery in terms of months and years and often work to scheduled, cyclical delivery profiles (this generally means a smooth delivery profile).

    Compare that with after-sales, where the use of a product is likely to be highly variable across the customer base. Consequently, the consumption and/or failure rate will be equally variable. Furthermore, customers usually prefer to minimize their inventory levels. Hence, when they need a spare or an item for MRO, their delivery requirement can be measured in hours or days.

    To provide context for the importance of timely delivery—the immediacy of usage in after-sales, means the focus is always on replacing or repairing an existing in-service product, making the speed of fulfillment that much more critical.
- **Inventory and Forecasting**
The OEMs have long-range delivery forecasts, fixed months, or even years into the future. They have 100 percent accurate bills of material (BOM) when making new products, as they use the same set of parts for every item built. These benefits simplify the inventory planning for the production equipment significantly. Indeed, both factors can permit them to utilize a

just-in-time (JIT) inventory management strategy, meaning that OEMs typically hold on-hand inventory only to support their immediate production needs.

After-sales must hold its own inventory to support its customer base. However, the customer requirement for off-the-shelf availability, combined with the unpredictable parts demand for spares and MRO, plus the multiple current/historic product lines, means their forecasting is significantly more complex. As a result, the associated inventory will typically be an order of magnitude higher than for the OEM.

Despite all of this, many OEM businesses fail to fully understand the clear and very marked differences between the two sides of their organization and insist on a common ERP system. This usually stems from three main reasons. First, the organization's c-suite utilizes the design and production facility's ERP. Second, they prefer uniform reporting throughout the entire business. Finally, convincing the OEM side to allocate further resources toward dedicated after-sales ERP investments can be an arduous one. This is primarily due to the complex nature of quantifying the costs associated with future suboptimal outcomes.

Further, companies also have a general unwillingness to openly acknowledge the necessity of planning for shortfalls and potential failures. This is particularly true when companies were sold their current system as a "complete business ERP solution."

So, despite the significantly increased complexity of managing an after-sales organization, they often find themselves left with an inappropriate business system.

I am not saying there are no ERP systems in existence capable of satisfying the needs of both sides of an OEM organization, because there are. However, in my direct experience, the very best after-sales organizations have been those with their own dedicated ERP, plus complete operational independence, and a clear location separation from the OEM side of the business.

But that is enough about the OEM world; as for an independent business, there is cause for celebration. As an independent, you will make your own decisions, and, consequently, you are significantly more likely to purchase an after-sales dedicated ERP system. Furthermore, you will not have to deal with the dominance of an OEM in your operation.

However, the problems associated with ERP systems extend beyond just OEMs, as neglecting the implementation of an appropriate system is not uncommon for independent organizations as well. Based on my experience, this is usually due to the presence of an outdated legacy system that was once efficient but has not undergone substantial updates or modernization. Operating in a business world that is constantly changing effectively leaves such systems hopelessly out of date.

Regardless of the business type, successful identification of the right ERP, whether that be updating and modernizing existing, or purchasing brand new, ultimately hinges on conducting thorough due diligence. It is crucial that all stakeholders explicitly define their needs and desired outcomes; the ultimate decision-making body must acknowledge and accept these.

The following are two examples of how businesses can get their ERP decision-making wrong:

One organization was aligning their various disparate businesses under "one roof," to effectively provide their customers with one point of contact for all their after-sales requirements. Each of these businesses had their own distinct legacy ERP system in place, so they hatched a plan to replace these with one overarching system.

Because of significant concerns, the after-sales team presented to the board their doubts about the suitability or "modifiability" of the OEM's existing ERP system to meet their present and future needs. The board subsequently directed the team to conduct a project evaluating four distinct ERP systems and present their findings.

The formation of a team comprising essential stakeholders marked the beginning of the due diligence process. This project aimed to evaluate the potential systems, including three that were specifically developed for after-sales purposes, and the fourth being the OEM's current system in use.

It took approximately four to six months for the review process to be completed before it was ready for board review. One clear winner was identified by the results, while the existing OEM system ranked a lowly third or fourth, with a significant and crucial gap between it and the first-place system. The "winning" system was first when measured against every line of the review criteria, and this result created a significant sense of anticipation and excitement across the whole after-sales team.

Following the completion of the project, the team presented their conclusive report and recommendation. However, after consideration, the board rejected the nominated solution and instead emphasized the necessity of embracing the existing OEM ERP as the system of choice.

Of course, this response was very disheartening, especially considering all the effort that had been put into the process and the initial encouragement from the board to conduct the review. Consequently, it was hardly surprising that the outcomes were not positive—the team lost trust in the board, and there was wide-scale demotivation among the workforce. But critically, the system encumbered the after-sales team and prevented them from reaching their full potential.

The second example involved an independent after-sales organization that was using a 15-year-old ERP system. Unfortunately, it had also not been routinely subject to updates in line with the changing business requirements. Instead, faced with apparently "strong" financial returns, the leadership team had adopted a "if it ain't broke, don't fix it" attitude. But concerns were growing that results were not reflecting the opportunities for growth available.

Closer inspection of the business revealed that the ERP system was playing a major part in this. For example, basic order management required the use of nearly 20 different input screens/forms. The path between these screens was neither automatic nor intuitive nor "hyperlinked," and so the administration team faced having multiple display screens open at any one time. Data also had to be reentered many times across the ERP system architecture, leading to regular errors and subsequent lack of data integrity.

The inefficiency also resulted in the administration team being significantly larger than necessary for the level of business being managed. They also had difficulty keeping new staff because of the antiquated system, and their service level was both sluggish and suffering from regular failures.

So, just what are some of the key benefits that a modern ERP system can deliver? Well, a system that is well matched to a business can provide:

- Clean, efficient data entry and management.
- Human-led processes via intuitive and business-specific user interfaces.
- Improved productivity.
- Improved data security and accuracy.
- Significantly increased data visibility and access.
- Simplified reporting with "endless" user tailoring options.
- Regular updates and a simplified process for architecture changes.
- Access to *artificial intelligence (AI)* tools.

All the above can contribute to greater efficiency, accuracy, and speed and, ultimately, enable the delivery of significantly improved results to both a business and its customers. Effectively, having strong, efficient system foundations will allow a business to take greater advantage of the opportunities available to it and optimize its results.

Disruption resulting from any change is undoubtedly a truism, and, of course, there is considerable potential for this associated with large ERP rollouts. Undoubtedly, naysayers will talk about this as justification to maintain, or at best, tweak the status quo. However, sometimes, a "big bang," with a well-executed plan, can be an entirely appropriate approach for your business.

Ultimately, only you can determine what is the right path forward. However, it can also be too easy to focus on the "everything has to change at once' solution" and postpone or cancel necessary change.

I believe a famous general once said, "An army that prepares while marching will be significantly closer to the enemy by the time they are ready, than the army that does not leave barracks until it is 100 percent prepared." So, the fear of the negatives should never prevent action, as even the simplest ideas and changes, when well executed, can deliver incredibly positive results.

Similarly, never lose sight of the simple fact that an incrementally delivered solution can potentially reduce both the challenge and the risk to smaller bite-sized chunks.

In summary, it is worth reiterating that after-sales service levels will only ever be as good as the processes and systems that underpin them. So, any failure to resolve these issues can effectively undermine the future of a business.

Top Tips

- The best organizations will deploy *customer relationship management (CRM)* systems alongside (or as an integral part of) their ERP. This ensures their businesses are running at optimum efficiency and making the best use of all the market intelligence available to them.
- You may have already invested a considerable amount of time, effort, and cash in deploying the right system for your business. However, we live in a fast-moving world with an amazing speed of technology development; hence, you should never regard a business system as "fit and forget." Instead, regardless of whatever you have selected, it will need to be reviewed regularly to ensure that it remains your best and most appropriate option for the future.

Customer Relationship Management

In their book *Customer Relationship Management*, Buttle and Maklan (2015, 3–4) acknowledge the term "CRM" has multiple meanings, but, for clarity, this book uses it within an information systems context only.

So, just what is CRM? Well, it is an integrated database and set of tools that allow a business to manage as many aspects of their customer interface as they choose, in an up-to-date, live, and extremely efficient manner. It can provide both a central, single version of truth within a business and a centralized in-house encyclopedia of knowledge about their customers and competitors.

Despite these benefits, many CEOs and business leaders I have encountered express doubt and resistance toward CRM systems, citing a lack of persuasive justification for the investment. This is understandable because it can be difficult to measure definitively (in advance) the improvements that a good CRM can bring to a business, although it is not impossible.

Buttle and Maklan (2015, 341–342) agree and point out that establishing accurate sales growth, incremental profit, and ROI numbers only comes with the learning gained from customer engagement, proven service-cost reductions, and so on.

Because traditional methods do not adequately assess the (both identifiable and latent) benefits of CRM, they advocate for real options pricing models, which have a proven track record.

Crafting a winning business case is challenging; each project's success depends on the organization, market conditions, and, critically, board-level buy-in.

I was first introduced to CRM in the early/mid-2000s, and I was also a skeptic, questioning its need and viewing it as additional and unnecessary data input. In the intervening years, I have used multiple such systems and have experienced the extensive benefits first hand. Based on my many practical observations, I now fully respect that it has a critically important role in supporting the customer management process.

While there can be challenges associated with its introduction (as with any business change), I would also state unequivocally that the positives far outweigh any negatives.

The following is a simple example of a typical issue that a CRM can address. Sales and customer-facing teams frequently have their salaries and bonuses linked to their individual performance. This can often lead to unhelpful behaviors such as not sharing information and/or collaborating well. Instead, they may hoard their knowledge as a source of personal advantage and power. In doing so, they frequently harm both the interests of the organizations they work for and themselves. CRM effectively eliminates these harmful behaviors by securely storing and safeguarding essential data, ensuring such data are readily accessible (to all, or defined user groups) within a company.

The ability to access data easily is a significant advantage for any business. An efficient CRM generates comprehensive reports on various customer interactions, offering insights in multiple formats, such as regular customer updates, sales performance, forecasts, and customer satisfaction levels. Moreover, it allows for quick and simple customization of reports to suit the specific demands of the business.

You can probably gather from this that I now sit in the CRM convert arena. In simple terms, I have found that having readily accessible critical intelligence about my business operation, customers, and competitors provides a significant advantage. This knowledge can empower any business.

If you are new to or inexperienced with CRM and are considering its use, I highly recommend conducting a comprehensive evaluation. At this stage, you simply "don't know what you don't know," so do not limit your outlook or waste effort trying to define a budget or exactly what you need. Instead, I would recommend starting by simply approaching your customers and other local businesses to determine what they use and what they feel are the positives and negatives of their chosen system. If possible, also try to establish what your competitors use.

I would then start discussions with the CRM suppliers. Some of them will visit your business and make (no obligation) recommendations on what they could provide and how it could benefit you. Take advantage of these options to broaden your knowledge base.

Once you have completed your initial research, you will need to define answers to the following four questions:

1. What do I want to achieve now?
2. What features and capabilities will I want the system to deliver in the future?
3. What else might I want/need in the future (blue sky assessment)?
4. What I do not need/do not want?

Only when you understand the CRM capabilities and how it might benefit your organization can you build a specification, cost–benefit analysis, and, ultimately, a final budget.

By approaching the project in this manner, you can quickly and simply define exactly what you need and when and, importantly, what you do not want. It will also allow you to ensure your selection will be capable of the service/product expansion, including scalability as your business grows. Additionally, do not overlook what I have seen to be the primary challenges for a successful CRM deployment:

- Lack of a clear usage case/strategy: Define the vision of exactly what makes up post-project success.
- Data quality: If your existing data are not of good quality, then it will be a case of garbage in, garbage out. This means there may be a substantial data cleanup exercise required prior to CRM deployment.
- Employee support is critical: If the staff do not believe in the project, it will fail; therefore, clearly explain how CRM will improve their roles and performance.
- Training: Do not underestimate the level and length of training that will be required.
- Eyes that are bigger than the belly: Avoid trying to deploy too much too soon. It is much better to start with a successful core deployment and then incrementally add functionality to build on that success.

CRM pricing starts at what I would consider being very reasonable levels and increases in line with complexity and functionality. Most CRM suppliers offer a range of modular options, allowing them to cater to the needs of businesses of all sizes, from *small- and medium-sized enterprises (SMEs)* to large global organizations.

While there are many suppliers, as you descend the list based on market size, you may find that more features require the use of optional applications attracting additional charges. To ensure fair comparison, standardize pricing to objectively evaluate the true total cost across suppliers with different core offerings.

You may also discover that third-party applications are required to be "bolted onto" the CRM core to deliver the key features you want. This presents a potential risk of your chosen CRM lacking fully integrated core features. You certainly do not want to find that your selected system and the bolt-on apps are not working together seamlessly. Similarly, if problems occur, you do not want to end up stuck in the middle of a CRM/application supplier finger-pointing exercise as to which product is to blame.

So, you need to ask yourself whether any price variance gained from using a "cheaper" supplier versus the market leaders justifies the potential risks.

Should you decide to deploy a CRM within your business, be very cautious of anyone who suggests it would be a good idea to develop your own system internally. Just run away, really quickly!

I have seen two such internally developed and managed projects, and both were very expensive failures. The outcome in both cases saw the organizations end up purchasing off-the-shelf systems. Here are just a few of the self-build failure points I have encountered:

- Resources: You will use existing resources—presumably those employees all had jobs before and so how will they divide their time?
- Knowledge: Granted, you might not be starting at point zero, as you may already have some knowledge of CRM. However, there is a big difference between that limited knowledge and being able to build a fully functional and effective system.
- Timescale: Unless it is a simple build, anticipate years, not weeks or months, for a fully operational and bug-free product.
- Testing: You will end up having to test the system in your business, meaning you will experience the bugs, teething problems, and associated potential operational disruption first hand.
- Training: There will be a significant training requirement, and, if your staff have not used such a system before, this will be ongoing through both the roll-out phase and for some time afterwards. Who will do this (I refer you back to the first bullet point above)? This is relevant when you realize the existing major CRM suppliers have comprehensive user forums and extensive freely available online guides exist.
- Employee buy-in: Perhaps the most important element— your staff will undoubtedly know what is available in the

marketplace and so will already question the motives for a self-build. Second, every bug and difficulty the staff experience will reduce their confidence in the product. This will cause them to be less and less inclined to either fully adopt and/or use the new system.

My overall impression is that self-building is motivated by pride or the false economy of believing it will be less expensive than purchasing a readymade solution. Therefore, unless you just happen to be a software development company with the right skills and the spare capacity, it is not advisable to take on such a project.

AI and Chatbots

Another area of CRM to consider is how it will continue to be impacted by AI. McKinsey reports that AI deployments in service operations centers reduced costs by 30 to 60 percent and improved delivery quality (cited Smith et al. 2025, 71). My own observations of just how fast AI can analyze large datasets and present the results and insights to frontline staff confirm these improvements. In the past, such tasks would have taken many hours and even days to complete.

Within their research of a typical customer service representative (CSR) role, Daugherty et al. (2023, 2) identified 13 typical tasks dominated the workload. They then analyzed the potential impact of *generative AI* on each individual task. The findings showed four tasks remained unaffected and needed to be conducted by humans. AI could fully automate four tasks and enhance five others. Interestingly, they also identified five additional high-value new tasks.

These examples show how AI can significantly improve service quality and efficiency by automating repetitive tasks and freeing up an organization's workforce.

That said, I note that many of those businesses already using AI have, unfortunately, focused heavily on the cost savings gained from replacing human roles. For example, many are using chatbots and AI to replace customer service agents.

If my career has taught me one thing, it is that you cannot cut your way to growth. Indeed, my experience has proven that this is the lazy option based on short-term thinking. It is simply the easiest to implement and quickest to deliver financial results. But it is also a one-sided strategy as, for example, it does not consider the advantages of redirecting experienced staff into other roles, such as key account managers or inside/outside sales. These are changes that can and will deliver greater benefit than cost-cutting alone, as described above by McKinsey.

The bumpy introduction of chatbots proves that removing humans from the customer interface also does not guarantee success.

Despite their growing role in customer management strategies, a field study of 35,000 chatbot interactions at a telecommunications company showed only 34 percent achieved a satisfaction rating above 1 out of 5. Further field and laboratory experiments have shown that customers believe cost-cutting and profit optimization motivate the use of bots as opposed to delivering benefit to them as consumers. These two factors lead to lower customer satisfaction with chatbot support compared to human support (Boegershausen et al. 2023, 1–2).

In fairness, chatbots began as simple scripted (rule-based) responders severely limiting their capability, and I believe this experience continues to cast a shadow over their adoption and acceptance.

Over time, we have seen steady and significant improvement, and, today, chatbot capability is greater than it has ever been. The very latest versions use conversational AI, *natural language processing (NLP)*, and machine learning (ML) to deliver human-like conversational responses.

Consequently, chatbots have significant advantages over traditional human service agents. They are available 24 × 7 × 365, do not go on holiday, stop for lunch, or get sick. They can now handle complex issues and are able to provide faster responses. For international businesses, they can speak to your customers in multiple languages as opposed to forcing them to use your home language. Finally, they can deliver significant efficiency gains through automation. For example, one global organization automated nearly 70 percent of their customer service calls via virtual agents (Kannan and Bernoff 2019, 3).

Despite this, there remain challenges, and, in my experience, the most frequently reported frustrations still relate to the robotic nature of the interactions and customers being left "hanging" with an unresolved issue. These can occur in both rules-based and conversational chatbots. Essentially, the chatbot reaches either the "no" point in its script (rules based) or the limits of its knowledge/human characteristics (conversational).

We must also consider other employee and customer cultural needs and assumptions. For example, while customers in Asia are more accepting of robots than those in America, there is also a basic expectation for the human touch and "service with a smile" (Grandey and Morris 2023, 5). Consequently, I strongly agree with the assertion that a readily available, one-click option to connect with a skilled human agent is required (at least) until functionality has improved and customer adoption is fully demonstrated (Buell 2018, 4).

In the absence of any other information, employees will probably associate any talk of AI with efficiency and potential headcount reduction. So, not for the last time in this book, I recommend involving affected employees in the decision-making process. Instilling a sense of both ownership and empowerment and exposing employees to the benefits of how these new tools can enhance their performance will undoubtedly help to allay their fears.

These issues also expose the risk in the strategy of those organizations who become reliant on AI/chatbots to support their customers, without understanding (or ignoring) the current limitations of the technology, market, and employee acceptance.

That said, it is also very clear that the use of generative AI and *large language models (LLMs)* will continue to drive rapid improvement and extension of chatbot capabilities and performance.

With AI's increasing sophistication and the rise of tech-savvy employees and consumers, the trend of forward-thinking organizations partnering employees with machines will only continue to grow.

In the book *The AI Revolution in Customer Service and Support*, the authors present the following seven alternate future states for the impact of AI on customer service (Smith et al. 2025, 469–472).

1. AI will replace all human customer service roles.
2. A hybrid model where AI conducts most service actions, with customers having the option to engage a human for a premium price.
3. Humans and AI work as collaborative partners.
4. AI advocates deliver deeply personalized support to customers.
5. Human agents continue to provide customer service, supported by back-office AI coaches and consultants.
6. AI provides premium, highly personalized services, with humans providing routine support to those customers who prefer it.
7. AI cannot make the advances required and falls from grace, leaving human service agents in charge.

Based on where we are today, I think the first point to make is that the future advancement, associated timescale, efficacy, and customer acceptance of AI are all somewhat unknown. Furthermore, the diversity of customer needs and human nature makes a one-size-fits-all solution unlikely.

The after-sales marketplace is just too dynamic and varied, consistently inconsistent if you will, to be neatly classified in this manner. Instead, I believe the reasons variable support solutions exist today will continue to drive a mixed approach in which future states (1) through (5) will all feature to at least some degree. I also believe that future states (2), (3), and (5) will be the most dominant; future state (3), because it blends the best from both AI and human support; and future states (2) and (5) based on my belief that suppliers will recognize the competitive advantage of offering human-centered, personalized services. A premium service price would likely accompany both options, like current pricing for five-star hotels and first-class travel.

For completeness, I have excluded future state (6) because it exercises none of the efficiency opportunities that AI can provide on routine support. Future state (7) is also excluded simply because we have already moved passed that point.

The ongoing risk with any AI-based solution is that organizations seek to justify its deployment through a myopic focus on cost-cutting alone. A systematic approach, including thorough research, will better identify how AI and chatbots can most effectively improve after-sales service, rather than letting staffing cuts drive potentially poor decisions.

In summary, I believe we are still very much on a journey of exploration. Widespread AI adoption in customer service hinges on several factors: the technology's human-like qualities and interpersonal skills, its capabilities, and, ultimately, the acceptance of both customers and coworkers (Grandey and Morris 2023, 8).

Top Tips

- Undertaking a CRM design and self-build means you will reinvent the wheel and will undoubtedly end up experiencing all the trials and tribulations the existing suppliers have ironed out over many years. Furthermore, considering such a deployment emphasizes the immediate need, so why not explore an off-the-shelf solution? It will provide you with all the benefits significantly faster than a self-built solution.

- In the rapidly developing field of CRM, there is a seemingly never-ending and growing list of potential additional apps. So, if you choose to invest in a system, ensure that you also deploy a process for ongoing optimization.

- Do not rush into automated AI-powered after-sales support; fully explore the strengths and weaknesses of human–machine partnerships first.

- Do not underestimate the potential for coworker resistance to AI-based technology. Ensuring employee buy-in needs to form a key part of any deployment plan.

Data Management

While I am certainly no data management expert, I do want to briefly touch on the subject to deliver what I know to be salient points.

We all recognize that knowledge is power, and the more you know, the greater your chances of making the right decisions. Despite this, far too many businesses are still making critical decisions based on instinct or gut feeling simply because they do not have good quality, easily accessible data.

Every process step and point at which your business comes into direct and indirect contact with your customers presents an opportunity to collect data. Certainly, collecting this information will never be effortless. But even today, far too many businesses cannot grasp the value that this "freely" available data can provide if only it were being collected, stored, and used appropriately.

Businesses can automate and track internal processes while collecting external "offline data" such as newsprint articles, TV, radio, annual reports, and so on. However, much key data are already immediately available for automatic collection through both your internal daily activities and external interactions with your customers.

While it is fair to say that some ERP systems may provide some (or maybe all) of the internal data, this may not always be easily accessible or user-friendly. However, deploying a professional CRM can provide the foundations for a business to excel when integrated with an existing ERP and industry-specific applications.

Some forward-thinking after-sales organizations have made CRM the core of their business, streamlining customer-facing activities like sales, quoting, billing, and support through this efficient platform. This provides them with a centralized "one version of the truth." All the critical process and customer data have also become easily accessible and ready for both harvesting and daily usage within the business.

The following are two simple real-life examples of the transformational power that harvesting and analyzing data from systems such as ERP and CRM can provide:

One business that I also refer to later in this book had no real understanding of their customer *request for quotations (RFQs)*.

They improved this by reengineering the process and using their existing ERP, plus CRM to include clear steps and data collection points. As a result, the business identified their RFQ conversion rate was significantly below what they had understood it to be. This was hardly surprising given that they had not been collecting the data previously and so had no factual basis for their assumptions.

Post the changes and as they built their dataset, they came to understand exactly what was driving the issue. They identified that their speed of response to the customer was critical to success and there were also significant shortfalls in the inventory they were holding on their shelves.

By addressing these two issues, they had more than doubled their quote-conversion rate within a relatively short time.

The second business had identified their administration team was overwhelmed and simply ignoring (and deleting) many RFQs. By simply cleaning up their processes and adding data points, they could calculate an average RFQ labor processing time. Adding this information to the volume, they could quickly produce a data lead labor resourcing plan—something they could not do previously.

As expected, once they allocated the appropriate level of administrative resources, the company witnessed a substantial increase in sales simply by maximizing their responsiveness to RFQs.

Of course, these are relatively basic changes and improvements; however, they still delivered very impactful results to the businesses concerned. Worryingly, though, many organizations have failed to address such issues. Whereas the most successful businesses have understood the benefits of collecting and managing data and using it to gain actionable insights that drive progress, expansion, and risk prevention.

Over recent years, it has been frequently said that the best businesses do "Big Data," and, based on my observations, I concur. What do I mean by "Big Data"—the ongoing capture of significantly larger amounts of operational, customer, and market data.

These datasets can be vast and underpin activities such as predictive modeling, forecasting, and advanced data analytics. More varied data points can provide more complete answers and, consequently, produce better-informed decision-making and solutions to business challenges. Essentially, it is a very effective method to "clear the fog" that surrounds business operations, customers, and competitors.

In summary, if you truly want to turbocharge your results, you will need a significantly better understanding of your operations, processes, customers, and competitors. Great data management will provide your organization with timely, accurate, and easy-to-access information, enabling informed (factual) decision-making at every level. ERP, CRM, and Big Data sit at the very heart of that journey.

Top Tips

- Data provide the ability to move easily from emotion, instinct, and "gut feel"–based arguments, to factual positions. It should be of no surprise that most organizations prefer to deal with the latter, especially when implementing change and/or making investment.

Intellectual Property

There may be disagreement about the importance and longevity of *intellectual property (IP)*, and, indeed, Bill Gates, former CEO of Microsoft and philanthropist, said that "intellectual property has the shelf life of a banana."

In my professional career, I have observed that managing IP is critical when handling highly engineered and unique products; however, it is important to acknowledge the finite lifespan. Consequently, I believe IP protection should focus on the deployment of effective controls to maximize the longevity of its value to an organization.

Given its importance to many businesses, it should be a prerequisite that they look after and securely protect their IP. After all, if a business cannot protect its own information, why should it expect anyone else in the market to do so either?

Unfortunately, many organizations fail to recognize the importance of IP protection. In the following brief examples, I show how an organization I worked with lost control of theirs and how another turned it into a cash generator.

> The first business supplied technically complex products, and many of their customers wanted to service these either themselves or through independent organizations.
>
> The technical support staff were receiving many external requests for detailed information—for both parts and tooling. However, as discussed in previous chapters, the organization's lack of interest in after-sales, combined with no formal IP guidance or controls, left them rudderless and self-managing. Trying to be responsive and maintain customer satisfaction, valuable IP was being sent to external customers without charge, tracking, visibility, or limitations on its use.
>
> I observed the second business had a singularly more advanced view of the risks of IP control. Following some initial success in pursuing IP breaches and securing financial damages via the legal process, they set up a dedicated control team with its own specific sales target. Their aim was simply to chase down those organizations illegally using their IP and generate revenue from it.

In summary, if you have any IP, protect it. Having a clear control plan in place, with approved delegated authorities and clear commercial terms, will be a significant advantage.

Do not lose sight of the fact that, at the very least, IP represents a potential additional revenue stream either through outright sales, or ongoing licensing fees. So, it is advisable to establish a formal recording system for all technical inquiries, and CRM can serve as an effective tool for managing and organizing this process.

The CEO of Walt Disney, Bob Iger, made a very valid point when he said: "I've always believed that the best way you combat IP theft is making a product available that is well priced, well timed to market, whether it's a movie product, TV product, music product, even theme park product."

This principle applies to any business where IP holds significance. The more satisfaction customers have with an incumbent supplier's product, pricing, and service, the higher the entry barrier becomes for potential competitors to engage.

Finally, IP is the lifeblood of many businesses, and, therefore, its management is a business-critical factor.

Top Tips

- The question with IP breach is always *"how do you know who is doing it?"* and so here are some simple tips. If, for example, you are investigating IP usage across MRO, then the obvious areas to investigate are:
  - Your competitors' websites to identify which products they are servicing (capability lists, sales promotion information, etc.).
  - Which (if any) MROs are you selling spares directly to?
  - If you have official distributors, then negotiate to see their customer list for your products.
- Ideally, include a clear statement in any formal spares distribution agreement that outlines the requirement for the distributor to share the relevant product and customer data with your business. Once you have a master list of those MROs who are purchasing your spares, you will obviously be in a much stronger position to both assess potential breaches and start appropriate preventative action.
- Achieving a 100 percent effective seal to prevent IP leakage can indeed be quite challenging. Hence, it is crucial to keep in mind that exceptional service and customer satisfaction can effectively diminish the market space for potential competitors to leverage what IP might be available.

Product and Service Lifecycle

In terms of the dynamics of maintaining customer satisfaction in the lifecycle of any product and service, there are two key inflection points: *entry into service (EIS)* and sunset.

Entry into Service

It may take years to develop new products and services before they enter the market and get used. Ideally, the development team will have fully evaluated and tested every possible operational scenario, stress, and environmental impact. However, despite all the preparation, many of these projects will still have reliability/deployment teething issues that can lead to unexpected *infant mortality*. These issues can be anywhere from the very minor, to requiring major redesign.

Why does this happen?

Even the best and most comprehensive design specifications can simply fail to address the actual full range of conditions that will present themselves in real life. It is incredibly difficult to know how each customer, both domestically and internationally, will interpret and utilize the product/service, despite everyone's best efforts.

So why is this an issue?

Imagine that you have your new product recently launched to market and suddenly it fails unexpectedly or maybe the customers start complaining about performance. This relative "newness" to service could mean there are few spares available, and MRO might not have been forecasting an early influx of product.

Quickly after launch, it is possible to find yourselves with multiple challenges, including: What is the cause of the issue? How are we going to resolve the problem? How do we support the customers in the meantime with adequate spares and MRO? As a result, it is very easy to transition quickly from the euphoria of releasing a new product/service to one of major customer dissatisfaction.

Having experienced this pain, I can assure you that no customer is going to be satisfied with such challenges from their latest investment.

How do you go about preparing for these issues?

Obviously, you need to be designing good products and services in the first place, but how? The multidisciplinary team approach of *concurrent design* represents a major breakthrough, ensuring comprehensive knowledge integration in new designs (see Warranty Support).

Recognize and accept that, inevitably, there will be "escapes" (quality and design issues) that result in early-life performance challenges. So, unless you want your very own horror story, in the words of the bestselling author Stephen King, "there's no harm hoping for the best, as long as you're prepared for the worst."

As described earlier, I strongly recommend that your business prepare buffer inventory levels for any new product EIS to cover unexpected increased demand, including spares for direct sale or parts for MRO.

While no business likes to hold inventory "just in case," history has clearly taught us that EIS is a high-risk part of the lifecycle. Instead, it makes sense to hold additional emergency inventory during the early stages of product life. This can protect your business reputation if you suddenly cannot support your "bright shiny new thing." If in the future you have still not used the buffer inventory, you can simply decide to reduce new demand for stock until the market has consumed any excess.

The decision on how much buffer inventory to hold is always a question. Whatever you decide, it will only ever be an educated best guess. It is essential to note that proactive measures to address potential challenges during the initial service phase of a new product will significantly improve customer tolerance in the event of difficulties.

Sunset

As previously discussed, an after-sales business faces the challenge of covering a broad range of products. For independents, this can be a simple discretionary decision to include and exclude items from within their service range as they see fit. But that is not always an option for OEM after-sales services. The latter may face contractual obligations to support all legacy products or services their parent organization has ever created, even until their end of life. This can present a significant and expensive challenge.

How do you solve this issue?

Unfortunately, some "uneducated" OEMs try to instruct their after-sales division to cease support with no understanding of the external or internal implications for such a decision:

Moral and Contractual Obligations

Who else will support the customers if not them? Do not abandon them. Of course, those previously mentioned contractual obligations to support these products and services until their "end of life" may also be in force.

Margin Impact

The evolving market demands have brought about new products and services with more restrictive commercial terms. As a result, the older legacy products can generate significantly higher margins than the new products.

Loss of Potential Revenue

Customers may prefer to maintain their existing products and services as opposed to making a larger initial financial outlay on newer replacements. This provides for higher price, margin, and development opportunities.

Retrofits, Modifications, and Upgrades

Well-resourced and well-managed *retrofits, modifications, and upgrades (RMUs)* activity on in-service items can be a very fertile ground for additional sales growth. RMU can provide new features and product/service life extension opportunities plus openings to replace competitors' in-service offerings. These are options that can generate significant additional revenue streams.

There are many companies specializing in product and program divestment that can also provide solutions for lifecycle management. Such organizations can take complete responsibility by purchasing the rights, including design and manufacturing responsibility. Alternatively, they can purchase a license to be the support arm for the product range, with the OEM keeping manufacturing and design responsibility.

The key challenge for any business is to pick the right time for the divestment. Some want to divest too early without fully understanding the financial implications. Alternatively, there are those who try to maximize returns before divesting, but this rarely works out well as any potential acquiring company is left with limited ongoing value to support their business model.

There is always the ever-present risk of transferring the "secret sauce" (IP), especially when the divestment targets contain crucial technology that is still in use or related to new product design.

Palmer (2010, 241) addresses service divestment; his position is that every organization needs a systematic approach to the sunset phase of its services and products. To prevent decisions from being influenced by sentimentality, bias, and vested interests, he recommends a model that utilizes a weighted index to score critical retention factors, resulting in a data-driven ranking process. I agree. The risks associated with divestment and curtailment necessitate a thorough review of all factors before making any decisions. This will significantly improve the outcome. The alternative of either breaking off support or neglecting to establish a comprehensive management plan for current customers of your product is the worst way to foster customer loyalty in the future.

Top Tips

- Shortcomings in either the EIS or sunset phases of a product and/or service can create very significant negativity within current and future customer relations. Therefore, an evaluation of the risks to your business and customers before decision-making is vital.

Process

Throughout my career, I have taken part in many *business process reengineering* initiatives, ranging from small-scale departmental projects to large-scale organizational endeavors. In nearly every instance, we were able to pinpoint areas for improvement and subsequently enhance the efficiency and effectiveness of the business. This outcome is not surprising, considering the ever-changing nature of our customers and the markets in which we operate.

Adhering to outdated practices simply because "that's the way it's always been done" can lead to falling behind the competition. Therefore, you need to understand the importance of regularly evaluating and challenging the validity of a business's processes and operations.

However, just a word of caution relating to the large projects driven by the introduction of overarching management operating systems. Over time, I have witnessed many of this type of restructure, and, unfortunately, most of them have not achieved the desired, lasting improvements, despite good intentions.

The two most common failure modes have been the urgent need to drive everybody through the training for the new "system." Training is obviously no bad thing, but it needs to be deployed appropriately. Employees are not stupid, and they will easily see through training for training's sake, that is, box ticking, as opposed to giving them something meaningful to their roles.

The second and most important point is failing to deploy sharply focused and meaningful *key performance indicators (KPIs)*. In the event the employees cannot see or feel the predicted enhancements brought about by the new operational process, it can lead to a lack of motivation toward the change. Unfortunately, this can lead to significant disruption within the organization, further impeding the achievement of desired outcomes and exacerbating employee detachment.

In terms of specific process optimization, I have seen the *Six Sigma* tool kit deployed multiple times and always noted it to be a very effective approach. In fact, in almost all cases, the deployment of this tool resulted in valuable improvements in processes.

So, while you may think you run an efficient business, if you have never truly undergone such a surgical assessment, the outcome of such a structured approach may be a surprise. Moreover, making improvements before investing in automation for your ERP/CRM is best practice, as you do not want to simply copy existing flawed processes. Consider this a business revamp and great for establishing waste free operations.

It would be nice to think that organizations would fully understand and support the use of technology like CRM to improve their processes. However, that is not always the case. In the following two examples are organizations I have encountered that either already had CRM available or had senior management who were not supportive of its use:

1. The first example relates to an organization that had loosely defined manual sales opportunity management processes (sales, commercial, legal, finance, etc.). Without manual prompting, the lack of interaction between these processes caused regular late delivery and incomplete customer proposals, resulting in a negative impact on the win rate.

   Having accepted there was an issue, the management team began a project to look at the process. They soon realized that there were multiple points upon which they had no data to support the following:
   - Live visibility of opportunity progress within the system.
   - Proactive identification of any blockages.
   - The number of customer *request for proposals (RFPs)*/RFQs being received.
   - Meaningful staff workload targets.
   - Sales opportunity win rate.
   - "No quote" decisions.
   - Identification of new product and service opportunities arising from any "no quotes."
   - Reasons why bids had been "lost."
   - Analysis of customer satisfaction related to the process.

   Essentially, the after-sales management team lacked crucial information to effectively oversee important aspects of their business operations. Instead, they were relying on intuition and emotions to make decisions. As a result, what initially seemed like a minor sales problem escalated into a larger issue that, once addressed, would deliver substantial benefit to the organization.

   There followed a larger project to identify the desired future state—one that would effectively clean up the process shortfalls and plug all the gaps that existed. In parallel, they also decided to "automate" the sales opportunity process via their CRM.

The result was a well-defined and fully cohesive process, starting from the initiation of an opportunity to the finalization of a sale. Following this, they thoroughly assessed all the other functions related to the sales process. This included Contracts/Legal and the *opportunity review team (ORT)*. Subsequently, these were also connected to the new central sales process (see Figure 3.1).

Thereafter, every individual opportunity in the business became trackable. At each stage, they implemented system time stamps

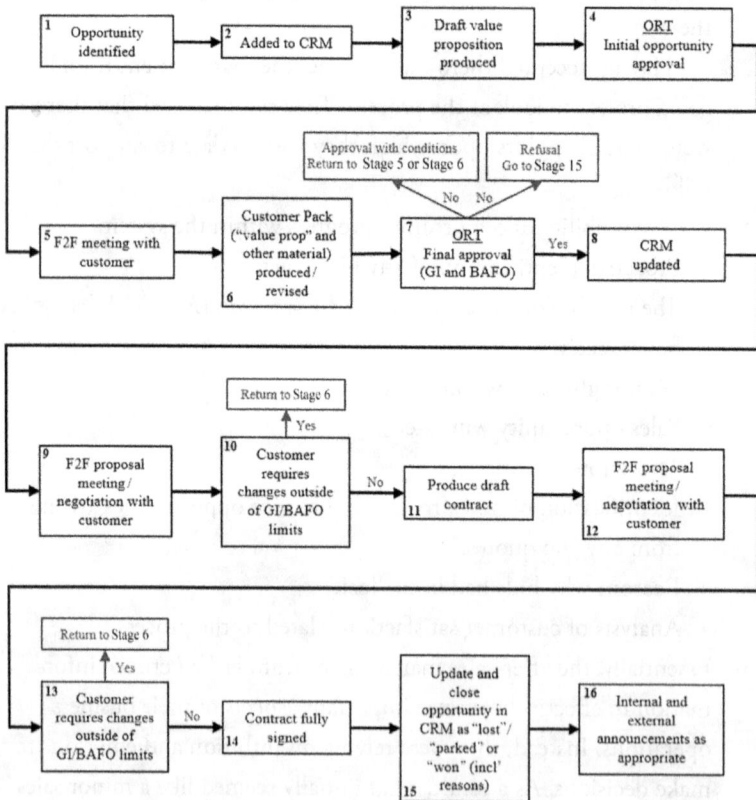

Key:
BAFO: Best and final offer.
GI: Going In.
ORT: Opportunity review team.

Figure 3.1 Sales opportunity management process

and automatic alerts for activities that were nearing their due date or were overdue. By simply clicking a button, they could produce real-time macro and micro reports, obtaining a full grasp of their sales opportunity status for the first time.

The result was a significantly more effective and efficient management system. Process lead times were reduced, proposal quality was enhanced, and the win rate increased.

This example's key takeaway: The organization already used the CRM within the OEM operation. However, they had minimal activity and effectively used it as little more than a Rolodex (aka paper-based address book).

The after-sales team wanted to use CRM, but there was insufficient management support because of misconceptions about complexity and cost. The core problem was the OEM's lack of understanding; they failed to recognize the value they already possessed and were paying for.

In the end, the after-sales team took charge of their own CRM deployment. They selected one of the existing senior customer support staff and tasked them with being the project lead. This individual lacked significant prior experience with such systems. But by eight weeks, using free online resources, they had progressed from being completely unfamiliar to something termed a "CRM superuser."

It is important to highlight that the organization successfully executed this project incurring no extra expenses, as their CRM module already included the support for process management. The only minimal extra cost incurred was for the extra "seats" needed for the additional after-sales users.

2. The second example involves a situation I have experienced with multiple companies. Upon investigation and analysis of the incoming RFP/RFQs, it was revealed that the customer service team was receiving hundreds of RFPs daily. It was also revealed that, because of their limited capacity, a substantial number of inquiries were simply being overlooked (and later deleted). The issue here was quite clear—on one hand, there was a business striving to increase their levels of inquiries and orders. To achieve this, they were deploying extensive external sales resources and expensive marketing

activities. On the other hand, their internal "receiving" team was blindly deleting a proportion of those potential growth inquiries!

In each case, the companies involved were operating with an outdated ERP system, with minimal reporting resources.

If I am being generous, I could accept the systems issue for the lack of awareness among the management team. However, it surprises me that there was no monitoring, even via manual data collection, for such a critical business function.

It is noteworthy that one affected organization, having become aware of the problem, refused to consider supplementary software (e.g., CRM) because of a perceived lack of value. I rest my case!

In conclusion, suitable and efficient systems and processes play an equally significant role in attaining optimal outcomes for your business. These elements serve as the fundamental pillars of your organization, making it futile to invest in costly ERP solutions without adopting a similarly forward-thinking approach toward your processes.

Top Tips

- Processes obviously need to be fit for purpose both today and tomorrow. It is not enough to adopt a "fix and forget" approach. Instead, while we should rightly focus all efforts on making them operationally sound now, we also need to adjust and polish them continuously to ensure they remain fit for the future.

Delivery and Schedule Adherence

It may seem obvious, but the simple fact is that if your business cannot supply your product and services either reliably, or at all, then effectively you will struggle to be the customer's supplier of choice. By comparison, suppliers who deliver on their promises with high reliability can achieve a significant competitive differential advantage in the marketplace (Jobber and Lancaster 2009, 96).

As we have previously discussed, a successful after-sales business relies on fast delivery and reliable, repeatable *schedule adherence (SA%)* with its customers, yet so many businesses struggle to achieve this simple feat.

It is not just about unreliable material supply chains, but also about other factors, like operating systems and processes, among others. For example, let us look at the core steps for a simple MRO process (see Figure 3.2). Even without considering the challenge of material supply chains, there are many opportunities for failure within each key step, not to mention the sub-processes involved.

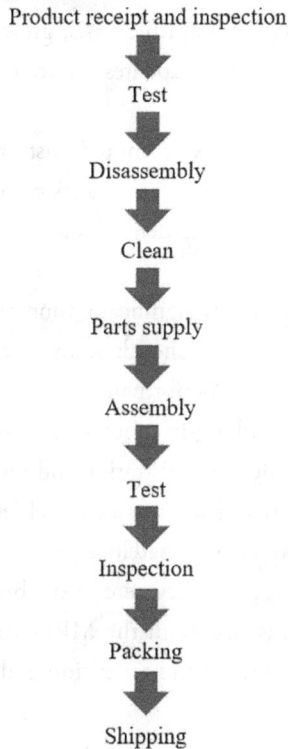

Product receipt and inspection

⬇

Test

⬇

Disassembly

⬇

Clean

⬇

Parts supply

⬇

Assembly

⬇

Test

⬇

Inspection

⬇

Packing

⬇

Shipping

Figure 3.2 Simple MRO process

Great internal processes are crucial for successful business operations, and, in cases like the one mentioned here, visual management has proven to be highly effective.

One MRO organization introduced a system that presented every in-house job on large screens in key areas of the business.

The system had automatic timers for each job, which activated a color-coded flagging system to represent different levels of urgency, including expedite and critical. These deadlines were based on customer delivery due dates and product progress. This was invaluable to the shopfloor to plan their workloads and spot critical items.

It proved equally useful to the customer service team as it provided clear definitions for each of the process steps, rather than just an overarching bucket called "shopfloor." Consequently, they could understand exactly where each of the customers' products were in the process on a real-time basis, greatly improving their ability to provide accurate updates in response to customers' questions.

Finally, automatic alerts prompted customer service to take proactive steps in resolving delivery issues by identifying items at risk of missing their projected delivery date.

Some organizations will focus significant time and effort on reducing waste and inefficiencies on their shopfloor and then overlook other areas that are critical to the overall performance. For instance, how efficient is the goods receipt and "booking-in process" in MRO? In spares distribution, do the customer order administration and the activity to pick, pack, and ship run in a series (inefficient) or a parallel (efficient) process?

All too often, delays in these satellite parts of a process can undermine all the best efforts spent elsewhere in the business. Whatever your answer, the good news is that both the MRO and spares processes are generally areas of high volume and repetition and so lend themselves to optimization.

Top Tips

- When analyzing your key processes, always review them in totality—from start to finish and include any "satellites" upon which they have any dependency. In this way, you will consider the customers' perspective, as they only experience the output of the entire process.

- As discussed earlier, measuring your performance at the overall level is required, but doing so at the individual process step level is best practice. Having measurement and relevant KPIs against all the steps in a process will both allow routine monitoring and quickly highlight any roadblocks that may (will) appear.

- If your business routinely operates with a high level of general disruption that comes from managing poor service, you may be carrying excessive resource to deal with this.

   Running a smoother, more efficient operation can also deliver headcount reduction via a smaller, more effective workforce. Alternatively, in markets with volatile demand, reducing the impact of managing poor performance can effectively provide the resource buffer needed to cope with peak customer demands.

   This is a prime example of using capacity management to prevent customers from taking their business elsewhere (Clutterbuck et al. 1993, 115–119).

Sales and Operations Planning

A significant number of the MRO and spares after-sales businesses that I have seen continue to transact the forecasting of their business in silos. By this, I mean each team operates independently. The sales team forecasts their sales activity, the shopfloor forecasts headcount and tooling, and the inventory team forecasts parts for distribution and/or MRO activities.

Sometimes, there is literally no (or very limited) connection, or discussion, or mutual agreement between these individual departmental views. However, if the various parts of an organization do not align, or behave in a dysfunctional manner, it creates a recipe for poor performance.

Sales and operations planning (S&OP) is an integrated process that brings all the individual departmental forecasts together but, importantly, ensures they are all aligned, reviewed, and agreed around the sales demand forecast.

How many times have you heard operations state "But the sales team are bringing in orders for the wrong products"? Often the sales team will respond, "But operations keep making and stocking products we cannot sell." This type of situation illustrates a lack of connectivity. However, S&OP greatly enhances communication and collaboration across departments, and it ensures a business has the resources (human, inventory, and machinery) to execute their plan.

While S&OP is more commonly used by larger businesses because of its complexity and resource needs, the fundamental practices and outcomes of the process are helpful for all businesses in attaining optimal results. Therefore, it is important to tailor the process to fit the specific needs of your business.

One facet of S&OP that I have seen businesses struggle with is how to break down the higher level product demand into the individual piece parts for MRO. For example, the sales team may estimate the repair of 20 Type X washing machines, but the challenge lies in determining which specific spare parts to stock to ensure prompt completion of the repairs.

In new manufacturing, they extensively use bills of material (BOM). But, since they build the same product repeatedly on a production line, the BOM remains the same—essentially it is 100 percent of the parts list.

However, in MRO, there is high variability—inconsistent parts wear rates and failure modes, and the customer can also introduce further unpredictability through their inconsistent use of the product and its operating environment. Therefore, the after-sales facilities will use a *proportional bill of material (%BOM)* constructed against their MRO experience to reflect the likelihood of each part needing to be replaced during the repair process.

For brand new products with no previous MRO history, producing a %BOM can be a significant challenge, as you are effectively trying to predict the unknown. In such cases, you have the option to seek guidance from the original design team, or perhaps you are fortunate to have engineering estimating resources.

Whatever the solution may be, it is highly probable that an inventory buffer will be required to cover any potential inaccuracy. On new items, such buffer inventory will typically comprise a significantly broader coverage of the potential parts and at higher usage percentages. As the team gains experience with the product over time, they will have more clarity on actual parts usage rates, enabling them to fine-tune the %BOM to reflect reality.

While having to hold additional inventory "just in case" is never a great position, doing so during the early service life of new products is critical. A buffer of inventory will permit you to address not only any inaccuracies in the %BOM but also any potential early-life failures (aka infant mortality). The very last thing you want to do is have your service fail on a brand new product—that really is not a good look!

Any modifications to the product that impact the parts used will also need to be reflected in the %BOM. Similarly, if any such change affects the fit, form, function, or price of the MRO, certain customers may opt to maintain their existing products without incorporating the modification. In such cases, you face potentially splitting the install base into pre- and post-mod %BOMs. This adds a further level of complexity both at this level and, of course, to the sales team's forecast.

As I have already mentioned, sales and demand forecasting can be very challenging in industries with after-sales that contain high variables. The following is a great example of how those variables can impact the availability of parts:

> Let us assume that your %BOM is 90 percent accurate, and your supply chain is delivering parts into your inventory with an SA% of 90 percent. Here, the combined probability shows an 81 percent chance of having all the necessary parts for the product (90 × 90). Assuming the demand forecast from your customer is 90 percent accurate, your overall forecast accuracy would drop to 73 percent (90 × 90 × 90).

Despite working in organizations with excellent data sources for their product reliability and market intelligence, the highest forecast accuracy I have ever seen is around 80 percent. But, even then, the figures were consistently inconsistent. This comes back to the point I discussed earlier, and that is simply the fact that no business has control of all the external factors that can directly impact any forecast and, by extension, the supply chain.

For the MRO shopfloor, the benefits of an accurate demand forecast are obvious. If management has clear visibility of the "what" and "mix" of products they are expecting, they will plan their resources (human, lean lines, tooling, and test) around that demand.

Investment required for new or significant growth in existing products will become clear, as will any end of life/cessation. Similarly, if the inventory team has a clear line of sight to the profile of both the MRO shop and/or customers' spares demand, they will plan accordingly. This will at least theoretically ensure the right inventory is in the right place at the right time (manufacturing delivery performance permitting).

In summary, having already established that forecasting is an inaccurate process, it would be unwise to rely solely on its use within S&OP. Instead, additional complementary strategies are required. For example, for inventory issues, these might include buffer stocks of parts and pools of completed products.

Having such additional inventory on hand to maintain both on-the-shelf availability and meet your delivery commitments will also require proactive oversight to prevent stock levels from getting out of control. Alternatively, it could mean ensuring that your shopfloor resourcing plan includes capacity for surge demand versus forecast.

Top Tips

- Just like a product forecast, %BOMs are not likely to be set in stone. Instead, updates throughout their life will be necessary because of external factors such as product age, parts failure rates, and modification actions.
- Some people believe S&OP is only about forecasting and inventory, but that is to do it a disservice. Do not lose sight of the simple fact that having great S&OP can provide a business with a competitive advantage. It enables businesses to enhance internal collaboration and supply chain, reducing inventory costs and increasing availability. This ultimately leads to higher customer satisfaction levels.

Key Performance Indicators

The management guru, Peter Drucker said, "You can't improve what you don't measure," and there is so much truth in that simple statement. That said, many organizations will focus their measures on the deliverable product or financials, for example, receipt of customer order to dispatch timescale, or actual sales versus predicted sales. However, if you look at a business in its entirety and realize that failure anywhere within that organization can and will adversely affect performance to its customers, you can understand why some businesses adopt a fully customer-centric strategy.

One business I have experience of wanted to bring in greater customer awareness and focus within their organization. They recognized that each function and process within their business was in fact a customer of and supplier to the next link in their delivery chain.

The internal supplier–customer relationships were formally recognized, starting a process where each function assessed its internal suppliers and customers based on specific criteria.

This is a very similar approach to the star rating system proposed by Heppell (2015, 2) although in their case they used a basic spider chart to present their findings. To the dismay of senior management, these findings brought to light previously unknown interdepartmental tensions, challenges, and setbacks.

Completing such an exercise prior to defining KPIs can be a very useful method of ensuring they are targeted on the most important elements of your business. Furthermore, it must be recognized that some measures may be inherently transient, addressing specific issues that are subsequently resolved.

KPIs really should be a basic, foundational feature in delivering after-sales excellence. However, even to this day, I see many organizations that either do not use them, or that have poorly focused measures, for example:

- They attempt to be too clever, resulting in excessive complexity and unwieldiness.
- They try to measure too much.
- Instead of aligning the KPIs across the business, they fail to do so and consequently often end up driving contradictory and unhelpful behaviors.

- Despite the best intentions of copying KPIs from other businesses, the importance of tailoring them to their own specific
  needs is often overlooked.

Ultimately, businesses should create KPIs at all levels, ensuring that they are
SMART—Simple, Measurable, Actionable, Relevant, and Time bound.

The benefit of having KPIs is to drive visibility and knowledge of how
your business is performing against its goals and to provide a clear direction of travel. They will also help to drive the actions and performance
of your employees. However, one of the key issues is that if insufficient
time gets allocated to their design, they can end up driving the wrong
behaviors.

Accordingly, you need to be wary of both the law of unintended consequences and to remember the adage—"We are what we measure." The
following are two examples of these points and their associated behaviors
in action.

One organization I worked with was struggling to get their MRO
performance under control. Traditionally, they had measured their
average *turnaround time (TAT)* at the highest level—essentially for
the entire business. However, with customer complaints growing
about both this and their delivery SA%, they deployed new KPIs
focused on both. These extra measures also flowed down to each
of the product-specific cells within the MRO shop to provide
greater granularity on where the issues were. After a couple of
months, the financial department reported that work in progress
costs were soaring, and nobody could understand why.

The subsequent investigation revealed that the shopfloor had
identified the negative impact of shipping items that had missed
their TAT delivery dates were having on their KPIs. As a result,
they simply halted all further work on any job that was overdue
and just ignored them!

Essentially, the MRO shop was refocusing their efforts on only
those items they could ship within their TAT and SA% targets
to ensure they maintained their KPIs. Unsurprisingly, this action
resulted in a steadily growing overdue backlog and increasingly
irate customers.

A second organization had implemented a suite of KPIs covering all its various operational areas. These measures included a revised and significantly reduced end-of-year inventory target (delivered straight from the board), with the bonuses of those responsible for its delivery directly linked to it.

As the year progressed, it had become clear to the inventory team that despite their best efforts, they would miss their target unless they acted. As the business approached the start of Q4, the team stopped raising any new inventory orders.

Like the above example, they did this in isolation to the rest of the business, and it was not until later the truth was revealed.

Regrettably, the lack of on-the-shelf inventory meant the MRO and spares teams failed to meet their growth targets, and there was a rising order backlog.

In fairness to the inventory team, they faced significant pressure from the board, leaving them with limited options. Unfortunately, the late identification of the issue resulted in inadequate time for processing and fulfilling manufacturing orders. Consequently, while the inventory team achieved its year-end objective, the organization's overall annual sales target remained unmet.

These are great examples to illustrate the law of unintended consequences. Poorly thought-through KPIs can lead to unhelpful management decisions. Here, both customer satisfaction and financial implications were being disregarded, by self-serving decision-making.

In the first example, once we discovered the issue, a simple solution was implemented, comprising two additional KPIs. One measured the average age of all the products within the shopfloor, while the second measured the quantity of units received for MRO versus the quantity shipped. By adding these two simple complimentary measures, we negated the original metrics' "hiding places" and provided a clear picture of the MRO shop performance.

The second example shows how poor management decisions and dysfunctional behavior at board level caused self-inflicted wounds to the overall financials of the business. The unfortunate reality with such events is that they can creep up on you and end up being singularly more painful to resolve than the original problem.

In these examples, it took the businesses about another five to six months to recover from the damage done and clear the decks of all the overdue items. The recovery from the customer dissatisfaction and reputational damage took significantly longer!

So, time must be taken to align KPIs and ensure they complement the overall business strategy and targets. Fail to do this and I can guarantee that loopholes will be found and exploited. This can be particularly true if companies connect the measured performance to their employees' personal performance reviews and bonuses.

If you are already running, or thinking about introducing a suite of KPIs, then my recommendation is to consider a balanced scorecard approach. This method provides a framework that will effectively translate an organization's vision and strategy into a fully aligned set of performance measures. Importantly, these will not just be financially based and therefore lend themselves to being applied across all areas and functions of a business. Ensuring full alignment of the measures means everyone in the business is focused on achieving a common goal (Kaplan and Norton 1996, 24–25).

In conclusion, if you do not measure, you cannot determine what is good or bad, and, without analyzing critical areas, you simply cannot achieve reliable, informed decision-making.

Your business is far too important to be left to run on emotion and hearsay. Customers, employees, and investors/shareholders are all depending on you and your business to operate effectively. It is, therefore, essential for everyone to fulfill their responsibilities to achieve this.

Top Tips

- Thoroughly think through the implications of any proposed KPIs. Once deployed, designate a slot in routine management performance reviews for critical functions to present their critical metrics.
- Ensure a full status accompanies any "red" scorecard/KPI performance. This will remove any hiding places and force your teams to address and confront the issues they face proactively.

CHAPTER 4

Communication and Customers

Having discussed customer feedback, it is now worth asking ourselves exactly what we expect from a supplier when we make an arm's length purchase. Even in e-business interactions, there will be a human involved at some point, so the transaction will still be subject to at least some basic human expectations. These include the need to be informed about the supplier's receipt, progress, and shipment of an order. Let me break down the individual elements of that communication:

- **Receipt acknowledgment of RFP/RFQ/Order**
  Presenting a simply stated "thank you for your order" message is basic good manners. Note that many customer purchase orders refer to their own Ts and Cs, and these can be very onerous. Therefore, in B2B transactions, it is always best practice to acknowledge a customer order as accepted against your standard Ts and Cs.
- **Confirmation of order acceptance (and potentially the projected dispatch date)**
  If you can acknowledge not only the initial receipt but also the acceptance/approval of a customer order and a potential dispatch date, this will be a significant positive.
- **Confirmation of any problems with the order**
  Silence is never, ever golden regarding the notification of issues with an order. Of course, customers may be upset and complain about order problems, but trust me, that will be an order of magnitude lower than if you offer silence.

    Forcing a customer to chase you for information is just poor practice. Indeed, a significant number of customers readily accept delay notifications, as being informed in advance at least enables them to plan proactively. Customers do also understand that sometimes the "wheels fall off the wagon," and they will recognize you have had the courtesy to engage with them.

- **Confirmation of order dispatch including shipping details as appropriate**
  The final stage in the process—why would you not want to let your customer know their order is on the way?
- **Summary status reports**
  If you have major customers with many ongoing orders and inquiries, it is advisable to provide summary status reports regularly. Such reports should include the in-house status of all the customer's live orders/inquiries, plus shipping data on their recently dispatched orders. Of course, if you possess a fully integrated e-purchasing system, then it should fulfill this requirement automatically.

The reality is that people are at the end of any order and people like to communicate. It is also worth noting the above points can equally apply to any transaction between a supplier and a customer, for example, order, inquiry, complaint, and so on.

Also, do not forget that in B2B your customers will also have organizations and bosses that require updates from their teams. Therefore, the more useful information you can provide proactively, the better prepared your customer contacts will be. Furthermore, if their own organization considers them a reliable and competent individual, assisting them to achieve that only serves to strengthen your personal and business relationship with them.

In terms of the "art of communication," there are plenty of books to help with this often-sticky area. However, business guru Tony Robbins sums it up effectively: "To effectively communicate, we realize that we are all different in the way we perceive the world and use this understanding as a guide to our communication with others."

Experienced business professionals often have a list of communication pitfalls. Here are a few golden rules I have developed over the years. They may seem somewhat obvious, but you may be surprised by just how often people fail to apply them.

Over-familiarization

Be cautious about being too familiar, especially in writing. Your contact may not appreciate it, and you never know who might read your e-mails, as many businesses have shared e-mail inboxes.

Humor

What might seem funny to you is not necessarily going to be funny to your customers, and this is even more likely if they are from a different culture. Also, your first language may not be theirs, leading to the risk of lighthearted, well-intentioned comments being misunderstood. So, be very careful of using humor in writing and always try to limit its use until you really know your customer and, even then, operate with caution.

Frustration

At some point, a customer will frustrate you—it is just what they do—some will even do it intentionally (most will not). Some of your customer contacts may be driven by internal instructions they might not even agree with but have no authority to ignore. To prevent escalating the situation, pause before sending a response. Take a breath, count to ten, and consider following these four tips that I always use in similar situations:

1. Try to have an off-the-record discussion with your contact to find out what is driving their position.
2. When creating a written response, it is helpful to produce a draft and then pause for a period before revisiting it. You will be amazed at how this gap can defuse potential knee-jerk reactions.
3. To gain insight into the customer's position, try to see things from their perspective and assess the planned response's acceptability as if you were the customer.
4. Have a colleague read through the communication chain as a fresh pair of eyes may uncover what you cannot see.

When writing, remember to avoid including anything that would make you uncomfortable if someone other than the intended recipient was to read it. In fact, this applies to both customers and colleagues within your own business. It is easy to send a hasty response and regret it later or make the customer even more upset. Therefore, exercise caution and only click "send" when you are completely satisfied.

My observations are that with customer orders, the best suppliers tend to over rather than under-communicate, and, if customers feel overwhelmed, they will let you know.

Finally, never forget that customers have a choice and so always treat them with respect.

Top Tips

- Being caught up in daily business tasks can mean overlooking simple, cost-free solutions that can greatly affect business relations. Two great examples involve teaching your staff to:
  1. Smile while talking on the phone as it changes the mood and creates a positive atmosphere. While you cannot see a person's body language on the other end of the phone, you can certainly sense their mood (Heppell 2015, 103). I must admit I was very dubious when I first heard this, but during a period of customer service training, we carried out blind testing. In a series of 50 test calls, we determined that over 90 percent of the "customers" successfully identified the "suppliers" smile, and they rated the interactions more positively.
  2. Always say a simple "Thank You" to customers (and colleagues).

  These two simple approaches will guarantee you positive results. While it may not have a quantifiable sales value, acts of courtesy and positive emotions contribute to your business's differentiation in customer service. Essentially, it can never hurt if your customers are referring to your business as "nice people to do business with."

Voice of the Customer

The primary and crucial point I want to emphasize is that "knowledge equals power." This makes it highly valuable to listen to, capture, and analyze your customers' feedback in relation to your business and the market.

In today's ultra-competitive and fast-moving marketplace, having a fully-fledged intelligence-gathering process on your actual and potential customers will be critical to success.

I have been involved in many sales projects, ranging from new product bids to ongoing after-sales support bids, from both OEMs and independent third parties. The key to my success has been taking the time to really understand the customers' needs (short, medium, and long-term), their strategic aims, and their challenges.

The construction of a well-rounded appreciation of your customers will better prepare you to comprehend, question, and potentially enhance their thoughts and outcomes, granting you a significantly stronger bid position. Simply put, if you are facing business competition, why would you not want your sales activities and customer relationships to have the best opportunity for success?

It would seem like an obvious choice to customize your sales and marketing responses to fully meet your customers' goals, even beyond their immediate business needs. However, not all organizations are as receptive or willing to invest the additional resources.

Having lived through many sales projects I would confidently state that the application of greater effort and thinking power does not go unnoticed externally. Although not a guarantee of success, this approach will make a positive impression on your customers and improve your position on the supplier league table compared to those who do not.

Aside from face-to-face discussions, one of the common methods used to improve an organization's knowledge of its customers are strategy and market surveys. Surveys are not a recent phenomenon, and I have been involved in their deployment since the early 1980s. Back then, it was typically a basic annual survey that went to the senior management within the customer base. We received the results, undertook some low-level analysis (by comparison with today's standards), and patted ourselves on the back if everything looked good.

Over time, it has become clear to me that well-constructed general business interviews and surveys with open questions about a customer's aims can be very revealing. Similarly, in-depth reviews of their publicly released material such as annual financial statements and investor reports and so on can be information goldmines. Essentially, these free sources can provide critical information that you can harvest and use to strengthen your knowledge and define meaningful action.

To fully implement best practices in this area, just include your competitors in the review process for a comprehensive understanding. You should also consider doing this for all existing and new/target customers regularly as strategies can change and external factors can drive quick course amendments to where businesses are heading.

Having decided you want to collect the data to support and improve your customer and competitor intimacy, what is the next step? Well, undoubtedly you can resort to standard business tools such as word processing and spreadsheet software, and these would certainly provide a very basic foundation. Having used these solutions through my career, I can confirm they work. However, they are limited in both their efficiency and ability to fully utilize the collected data. Additionally, to recruit and/or keep great after-sales staff, these methods are nowhere near to meeting today's employee expectations. Instead, businesses need to embrace more sophisticated approaches and stay up to date with the use of specialized software and AI analytics.

Customer Satisfaction

Another key element of your understanding within the *voice of the customer (VOC)* process is *customer satisfaction (C-Sat)*. Knowing how customers feel about your service and performance at multiple levels (senior management through to day-to-day working level) is critical.

In fact, a significant contributor to a customer's senior management view of any supplier will be driven by the feedback they receive from their own internal teams. In turn, these teams will manage both the day-to-day relationship and, importantly, the purchase orders with the supplier; essentially, they are the operations "coalface."

Additionally, strategic decisions by a customer's senior leadership may not always align with the reality of what is happening at the day-to-day operational level. For example, where no contractual relationships exist, or if contracts are nonexclusive, the customer's purchasing team may have freedom to choose who they send orders to daily.

Of course, it remains important to include customer satisfaction elements in intermittent surveys to senior management. However, the satisfaction score is primarily influenced by the volume of interactions at the working level. Therefore, it is critical for any business to know how their customers feel about them on a day-by-day basis.

After recognizing the importance of the VOC process and experimenting with different methods, I have settled on a tiered approach. This involves gathering feedback from customers at various levels and on different schedules. Routine scheduled (but intermittent) strategic surveys go to the c-suite. Usage surveys go to middle management, and order/inquiry generated *net promoter score (NPS)* surveys go to the routine daily contacts (see Figure 4.1). Sometimes, face-to-face discussions between strategic business managers and the customer are also used to make the discussions more personal as opposed to just something the customer receives by mail.

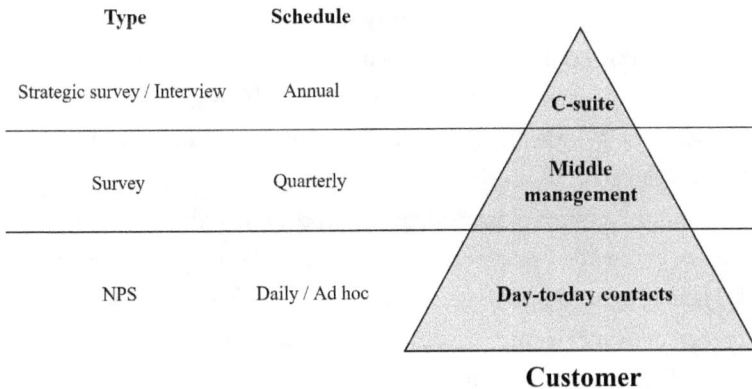

Type	Schedule	
Strategic survey / Interview	Annual	C-suite
Survey	Quarterly	Middle management
NPS	Daily / Ad hoc	Day-to-day contacts
		Customer

Figure 4.1 Tiered VOC strategy

With strategic customers, I have implemented regular *customer business review meetings (CBRM)*. These meetings merge and present VOC feedback as part of an ongoing joint scorecard. This higher-risk strategy means that any "red" (critical) issues are highlighted, putting the onus on early resolution. In fact, this is not a bad outcome as it encourages proactive behaviors within an organization.

So, an ongoing data collection from your customers to build a holistic picture is entirely possible and one that will be very helpful to your business. But many organizations lack the rigor for such an approach, and so a shift in attitudes and behavior would be the first hurdle to gaining such rewards.

To further support the case for such a change, here is another great example of the use and power of VOC.

A company I worked with had customer satisfaction issues at several locations, and by association these were hurting sales at their other sites (weakest link syndrome).

The company had previously implemented offline manual VOC processes at their different locations. However, these processes relied on inefficient spreadsheet-based tools, required significant resources, and had a monthly management reporting structure. As a result, the company was looking at everything in the rearview mirror, too late to have a meaningful impact on events. They eventually addressed the problem by deploying a multilevel customer VOC strategy, as outlined above.

For this example, we will focus on just one element. The organization recognized their many routine touch points with the customer were being inadequately monitored. They also knew they had to do a much better job managing and understanding customer service feedback. Ultimately, they deferred to the often said "you're only as good as your last sale," deciding they wanted something at "point of use." After review, they elected to use NPS methodology via the CRM that was already in place.

The first change implemented was the use of NPS within the customer RFP/RFQ process. The team set up a structure via the CRM that automatically created a "case" (a unique record) for all such incoming e-mail traffic. Each "case" would then be distributed to the appropriate workgroup for action. Customers received an automatic acknowledgment of their initial e-mail and notification when the action was finally closed. Upon closure, the system also generated randomly distributed NPS surveys.

Following the initial success, the organization extended this process to include all e-mail traffic and communications received via their website. They also started handling all telephone and hard-copy enquiries via the same route.

The positive outcomes of the addition of NPS and simple process improvements all managed via the CRM were:

- A live view of the health of their business via a constantly monitored customer feedback indicator.
- A formal mechanism for the customer to provide feedback on every single interaction.
- The opportunity to drill down into and address issues causing customer dissatisfaction on a real-time basis.
- Significantly reduced levels of customer complaint.

A final additional and not inconsiderable benefit for the business was an ability to analyze the total level of customer inquiries being received. As a direct consequence, they could improve workload planning and monitoring and accurately understand the required resourcing in key areas.

Initially, some individuals in the company doubted that customers would respond to the surveys. Even published data indicated that NPS response rates were typically only 1 percent. However, they consistently achieved around 5 percent, and this volume quickly allowed them to reach a statistically valid level of responses. This enabled meaningful automated reporting of customer satisfaction across the entire customer support function.

Along with implementing visual management, they showcased the NPS results on wall-mounted screens in their customer support centers worldwide. They accomplished this using a simple digital "speedometer" (red at one end of the scale, green at the other) to present a live view of the metric. Immediately, leadership could visually monitor the C-Sat on a real-time basis at their service centers, promptly analyze and categorize any negative feedback, and implement appropriate and timely resolution actions.

Top Tips

- Operating a business in today's market and not collecting and/ or using customer feedback is a high-risk strategy. Instead, the deployment of simple tools can provide that critically important and unique view of its performance from the customer's perspective.

Dispute Resolution

When working with customers, inevitably, disputes arise, and so it is important to have a well-defined process for resolving these.

One major customer frustration today is struggling to gain a supplier's attention for a complaint and experiencing unprofessional handling of the issue, as frequently reported in national press articles. Often, the supplier worsens the problem by failing to resolve the issue even after acknowledging and promising to handle it.

As I have discussed earlier in this book, customers will closely monitor how a business responds to a crisis or a thorny issue. The adept management of such problems can readily convert what might have been detrimental to a beneficial result. This supports the finding of Hart et al. (1990, 148–156) that resolving service problems can improve customer–supplier relationships and foster greater customer loyalty.

It is essential for any system set up to formally and visibly capture every dispute. They must be trackable, and there must always be someone responsible and accountable for ensuring the dispute is formally closed.

But even that is not enough, as again the news press has plenty of examples of customers saying that the supplier had closed their dispute with no resolution.

Therefore, the ultimate act of any dispute closure should be the collection of customer feedback.

To achieve this, I recommend introducing a process based on the previously discussed NPS. CRM-based dispute resolution systems are configurable to trigger the automated distribution of NPS surveys to customers upon dispute closure. While this would provide an instant point-of-use feedback as to the customers' satisfaction, even this might not prevent unjustified closure of a dispute.

Therefore, appropriate management oversight of the process will also be required to help drive the positive behaviors needed in this critical area of after-sales.

It is also very important to acknowledge and highlight the importance of disputes and their successful resolution to employees, customers, and other stakeholders. So, a business should ensure that it "walks the talk," by having the NPS dispute results added to the senior management KPIs.

A formal system of oversight and awareness is also necessary to preempt escalation of unexpected disputes to senior management. This system should include clear steps for internal escalation and review.

In summary, I have seen small and inconsequential issues quickly escalate into major incidents, with customers becoming even more inflamed because there is no dispute management process in place. To avoid walking an unnecessarily dangerous path, it is best practice to ensure deployment of a clearly defined and monitored system.

Top Tips

- When faced with seemingly intractable disputes, always try to arrange a meeting in person. I have found that it is significantly more difficult for customers to remain angry and belligerent when in a face-to-face scenario.
- It is important to walk in your customer's shoes. By doing so, you can assess the proposed solution and determine if you (and your team) would be satisfied if the complaint were yours. A negative response means there is already a clear indication of the probable customer reaction.
- There will be occasions when the customer issues you with a "take me to your leader" type request and demands to talk to your top-level management. This approach can be useful for showing the customer's issue is being taken seriously, but it also carries risks (see Negotiation). So, while this option can be an integral part of a successful dispute resolution, it will require very careful thought.

Lost Causes

It is true to say that the more customers you have, the more extremes of behavior you will see—that is just the natural rule of law. To tackle these challenging extremes, it is crucial to keep in mind the proverb "patience is a virtue." But in the after-sales arena, perseverance is another necessary trait that one needs to address this challenge successfully.

During my career, I have dealt with many customers who fall into the "lost cause" category. Essentially, this means there is apparently no hope of ever building or repairing a relationship with that specific customer and, more importantly, they do not wish to engage at any level.

There are many reasons to explain why customers might avoid your business. These could range from anything as simple as what they construe to be a rude e-mail/communication, personal conflicts, performance, or pricing issues and everything between.

Sometimes, these difficult relationships are resolved quickly, while others require patience and years of waiting for a chance to rebuild. For example, you may need to wait until the "customer blocker" loses their influence on supplier selection or indeed leaves the company altogether.

Switching the liaison staff member can also sometimes resolve the issue, and this does not suggest fault; a simple personality clash may be the root cause.

The following are two prime examples of lost causes I have witnessed:

- A sales team member at an organization visited a customer whose business had been inactive for a few years. Nobody knew why the sales activity had stopped, and so this was an exploratory visit. Upon entering the Managing Director's office and introducing themselves, the salesperson duly handed over their business card. The MD tore it up, threw it in the bin, and told them bluntly to leave and never to return.

  This was a prearranged visit and involved the salesperson making a 200-mile round trip, and so that was hardly an ideal response. The MD would not elaborate, and the cause of the issue remains unknown to this day. It was not until the MD retired

years later that the two organizations could restore normal business relationships.

- A few years ago, I was working with an organization invited to
attend a new *cost of ownership* conference series. Essentially, the
platform we and many other suppliers had products fitted to was
outdated compared to newer options. As a result, the end-users
were considering upgrading to newer and more cost-effective options from other suppliers. The conferences aimed to drive action
in reducing the operating costs of the existing platform, thus pro-
longing its use by customers.

  For the conference, each supplier was assigned a presentation slot during which they were to present their progress on
cost-saving activities. My colleague and I duly went on stage,
equipped with our view foils for the overhead projector (yes,
I know this dates me). We introduced ourselves and that was as far
as we got; one of the customer attendees stood and launched into
an angry, "fruity language"–laced complaint about our products.

  Regrettably, we were unaware of any specific dissatisfaction
among our customers and so were immediately put on the back
foot. This left us vulnerable and ill-equipped to tackle the issues
during our presentation. Thankfully, the customer eventually
burned themselves out, but not before others had also joined in.
Having endured the onslaught, we collected our material and
left to consider the reputational damage and "bruises" inflicted
upon us.

  Despite the customers' undoubted level of dissatisfaction, this
type of response was uncalled for. In fact, in today's world, with
the lowered sensitivity barriers and potential to cause offense, it
would simply be wholly unacceptable.

  We had three options—we could have met fire with fire, we
could have simply walked off mid-customer outburst, or we could
have listened and learned. We chose the latter, and it later proved
to be an excellent decision.

  Having collected all the customers' immediate feedback, we
returned to HQ, whereupon we set about the task at hand. This
involved further data collection from all the affected customers,

significant investigation into the products, and extensive activity with our OEM design team as we sought solutions. We were also speaking to the customers regularly as we tested theories and ran our assumptions past them.

These conferences were held every three to four months, and, when the next event came around, we were fully prepared and eager to take part. So, how did things turn out?

Well, the first point I will make is that it is amazing just how many people like to watch when things go wrong! When we entered the stage, it was standing room only in the auditorium as all the customers and other suppliers had squeezed in, hoping to see a repeat performance. We delivered our introductions and once again the customer stood up and in response we readied ourselves for a repeat. Instead, they said "Look, I think we may have been too hard on you last time and I apologize for that. But, as a show of goodwill, we have bought you both a gift." Upon opening our gifts, we found a t-shirt, each with a bulls-eye target emblazoned across the front. Cue much laughter all round and with the ice firmly broken, we never returned to the previous levels of negativity.

Our team closely collaborated with the customer base as the cost project progressed, and the program life was successfully extended. Eventually, when the platform was retired, this previously very dissatisfied customer purchased a replacement that featured a wide range of our products. Furthermore, we later collaborated with that same customer to create and complete an innovative "payment by the hour" contract, focused on in-service reliability.

So, there you have it—a furious customer who could easily have been regarded as a lost cause. Or we could simply have decided that because of their angry outburst, we did not want to work with them anymore. Again, making them a lost cause. However, our chosen route delivered a revitalized, close, and healthy working relationship, resulting in them becoming one of our most important contracted clients within a brief space of time.

Personally, it was a bruising yet rewarding experience. I learned a lot about myself and valuable lessons in preparing for conferences and handling irate customers.

The one unarguable truth is that after-sales is heavily customer focused, and, at some stage in your career, you will encounter a customer regarded as a "lost cause." What is critical to remember is that nothing stays the same forever: Today's lost cause could be tomorrow's Number 1 customer for your business.

Top Tips

- The challenge around the "lost cause" is to first determine why your business has a customer in this category. Once you know that, there are three further questions that will need answering before you can decide whether a "rescue mission" is appropriate:

  1. Do you need to, or want to, fix it? Is that customer important to you now, or could they be important in the future?
  2. How are you going to fix the problem? Clarity on the strategy and process required.
  3. What timescale and resources are required for the proposed fix? For example, this could include (i) the length of a negotiation and/or the cooling-off period the customer will require and (ii) any costs, for example, work hours and cash investment.

  Once you have answers to the above questions, you should be able to create a weighted list of customers, actions, and timescales.

CHAPTER 5

The All-Important Services

As you are reading this book, it is probable that customer service features highly in your organization's deliverables. Nevertheless, you might also have the misfortune of working in a company that perceives these externally facing roles impassively or, at worst, negatively. In such cases, there can be a simple misunderstanding that these jobs are of limited value and a cost burden to be endured.

I have noted this type of negative organizational climate in multiple settings, consistently leading to underfunding and understaffing of customer support teams and making them disproportionately vulnerable to job cuts.

However, and if we think logically, who in our organizations will touch the customer on a more regular and consistent basis than any other? The answer is, the "services" departments, including customer service/support, field service, technical/product support, and *key account management*.

The employees within these functions are the day-to-day face of a business, and, therefore, their structure and support directly influence how customers perceive a business. If you think that does not matter, then just read e-social media and daily newspapers to understand just how badly some of our major organizations are getting it wrong.

That many companies undervalue customer service by relegating it to the lowest levels of their structure and employing cheap, unskilled labor, it is hardly surprising dissatisfaction exists (Desatnick 1987, 7).

Now, maybe you have a truly unique product and enjoy 100 percent of the after-sales market and so feel less concerned about your customers' feelings. If that is the case, well done, but you will be in a minority of businesses that enjoy such an advantage. However, it is highly likely that even if you hold a dominant market position, potential competitors will be jealously watching and investigating how to gain a foothold. Therefore, caution is advised. This holds especially true if you are not delivering quality customer service, as in such instances, your customers may also actively encourage and enable new competitors to join the market.

Throughout my career, dominant market positions have nearly always been transient, which highlights the significance of neglecting customers. They are like elephants and will always remember how well you did/did not treat them.

That said, many customers have shared with me that one way they gauge a supplier is by observing how they handle a major crisis with their product/service. Such issues could be anything from availability, delivery, quality, and beyond. Indeed, some customers have mentioned that they did not really mind occasional mistakes because it gave them a chance to witness our recovery process in action. Essentially, the SNA-FUs gave them confidence in our ability to be a great supplier to their business even when the inevitable service problems arose—no matter whose fault it was!

In the following subchapters, I will explain some of the common issues and benefits associated with the service teams.

Customer Service

Upon assuming my first role as a customer support leader, it quickly became clear that the team faced challenges in providing cohesive, professional support. Moreover, their capacity to gather and maintain a thorough understanding of the market was limited. However, economic times were hard and so adding staff was not an option. Consequently, we set about looking for ways to upgrade our customer interface activities.

The project quickly identified that:

- There was a very fragmented silo approach to the customer support process.
- A small team priced jobs as the organization felt only they were qualified to undertake "specialist work needing years of experience." This was leading to a single-point failure mode and service delays.

- Other small, separate teams with different reporting lines existed for customer service, field service/technical support, warranty and sales.

Step by step, we introduced changes that delivered incremental improvement to our activities:

Centralization

Since all the teams were spread around the facility, we took the first step of creating a centralized customer support team with one reporting line. This brought together all the customer-facing functions into the same working area. Almost immediately, we saw significant improvement in the collective working environment and cross-team communications.

Collaboration

We also took the opportunity to discard all the old high-sided "pigpen" desks and instead introduced an open-plan workspace. Yes, there were concerns about noise levels, and it was certainly louder than the old layout. However, the improved team collaboration negated any drawbacks associated with the increased volume, and this was something that all the staff agreed on.

Multirole

Once we had the full customer support team co-located, we then took a hard look at the roles and responsibilities. I was convinced that by bringing the entire team together, we could streamline the day-to-day order support process. Before, three smaller workgroups took care of this, but with co-location we could transition staff into multirole positions.

Building Capacity

One of the key benefits identified was the removal of the repetitive single-point failure mode from each of the small work groups. The primary reason for this failure was the absence of staff due to training, holiday, and sickness. To address this, we planned to deploy a larger centralized, cross-trained team to improve load balancing and flexible surge capacity in the system. There were protests from some quarters, but after review, we proceeded.

Greybeards and Cross-training

Nominating specialists from each of the existing functions addressed valid concerns about skill sets and experience. These senior members served as the team's go-to advisers. We also put the greybeards at the center of all the structured cross-training activities.

Empowerment

We also wanted to unlock the power of the employees' skills and experience by empowering them to make decisions without constant reference to management. To support this, we established a *delegated authority* structure with clear ground rules. This enhanced individual responsibility and accountability for team members and reduced delays waiting for management. It also freed up resources that were then refocused on more important issues.

Management Support

In addition, we made it clear to the teams that errors were expected during the initial stages of the change. However, we assured them we would foster a "no blame" culture and offer complete support to those who learned from their mistakes. It is important to mention that practicing what you preach on this issue is crucial as unnecessary blame or criticism of staff during any such change will cause fear and a loss of trust.

These simple changes delivered positive results—we had created capacity within the outward-facing team, as well as delivering improved performance, collaboration, and knowledge sharing across the organization. Now all those previously unaligned functions were managing customers as a single team.

Was it a challenging time? Were the staff uncomfortable? Did we have difficult moments? Did we need to provide additional "hand holding" and oversight during the early days of post-change operations?

The answer is a "yes" to all four questions. But if you asked me if, with the benefit of hindsight, I would have done anything differently, the answer would be a firm "no." The positive results spoke for themselves, and we ended up with a stronger team. Moreover, there was a significantly higher level of responsibility toward customers, leading to much-improved job satisfaction. The dramatic improvement in service levels to our customers directly reflected in improved sales performance, and the customer support team became an area that others in the organization aspired to join.

I had learned that challenging the status quo is crucial when performance or results are suboptimal and when you have a better solution in mind. The argument of "but we've always done it this way" is only valid if "that way" remains the most effective approach, which is often not true. So, sometimes it can be very rewarding to take bold and seemingly anarchical decisions. Of course, as with any change, planning is critical, as venturing into the "unknown" without a clear direction and with no way of measuring the results is fraught with danger. So, a plan and clear metrics to monitor progress are an absolute must.

Key Account Management

As part of the operational review and changes described above, it was clear the customer service team was struggling to cope with the day-to-day volume of administration and support of the customers. Upon analysis of our customer base, we discovered that most of our sales were generated by a few large clients. In fact, many companies conducting a simple Pareto analysis will find that 80 percent of their sales come from 20 percent of their customers (Jobber and Lancaster 2009, 5). In our case, we also had a substantial number of very small clients forming a long low-value "tail."

Of course, customers all want to be treated as "Number 1," and so they do not readily recognize (or want to) their size of spend and relative importance to us as their suppliers. The result is that they all expect to receive similar levels of support. In our case, we realized we were dedicating most of our time and resources to managing the large number of low-value customers. Conversely, a significantly smaller amount of time was being spent on our largest and most important customers, and this simple realization prompted us to launch an urgent improvement project.

As it had become apparent that treating all the customers the same was neither efficient nor effective, we introduced a process of categorization comprising different levels or tiers.

The categorization process included individually scoring elements, such as strategic importance, revenue size, profit margin, quantity of orders, future revenue prospects, and so on.

The team totaled the results to create a league table, ranking customers in order of importance. We categorized our customers into three levels of service:

- A—for key, strategic, and/or the most important customers.
- B—for baseline, loyal, and profitable customers.
- C—for the rest.

We then directed the customer-facing teams to deliver sales growth through improved, focused customer support. The goal was to retain and increase sales with As, upgrade Bs to As, and either upgrade Cs to Bs or have them find a new supplier.

For the day-to-day administration, given that some customers are simply just "harder work" than others, we applied another set of scores differentiating them by their resource needs. These scores were based on criteria such as quantity of orders and inquiries; difficulty to deal with; level of complaints; payment profile; warranty issues; and so on. We subsequently created a customer league table, ordered by resource consumption.

Ultimately, this information was used to deploy a customer allocation with a balanced workload for each member of the customer service team.

These changes greatly improved customer satisfaction. Our business became simpler for customers to deal with, resulting in faster response and remedial times for any issues they had.

We never expected this activity to deliver immediate success, but our internal teams and customers quickly adjusted to the changes. Thereafter, we witnessed positive outcomes in a brief space of time, including:

- The business moved many Bs and Cs to a higher tier through service-level promotion.
- Improving levels of understanding and support for the As and Bs resulting in growth sales.
- A significant number of Cs moved away and became former customers of the business, leading to a reduction in the previous long tail of low-value clients. Despite this loss of clients, the tier project delivered a net increase in sales.

While this program was a success, we were also implementing the other changes to our support structure referred to earlier. If we had not implemented these parallel changes, the overall positive effects of the result would have been noticeably diminished.

The company also implemented a strategic key account management process, assigning a key account manager to each of its A class customers. This role served as the single point of contact for anything beyond day-to-day routine administration.

The strategic A class customers experienced significantly improved levels of support and communication through key account management. All of this resulted in a much more cohesive and open way of working between the organizations.

As we developed the process and became more skilled at managing our joint business interests, we made further refinements—and one of these changes involved introducing a formal CBRM. Effectively, this became the strategic review meeting that took place between us and our A class customers.

We worked together to develop the content and meeting schedule, building upon open tracking and reporting of the key metrics and concerns/issues specific to each account. Therefore, the CBRM structure and timetable were different for each customer. For example, if there were major issues in play, we might mutually agree to include new/extra KPIs and increase the cadence to a monthly review. Whereas, during times of relative quiet and high levels of customer satisfaction, we would keep the measurement package to the minimum "must haves" and schedule the meeting for every three to six months.

In terms of the content, the CBRM included subjects such as organizational updates, sales figures and KPIs, for example, paid/overdue invoice status, spares/MRO delivery performance, and technical issue updates.

The customer side of the report included elements such as quality and reliability issues, MRO and spares delivery performance (their view of our performance), and organizational updates.

Sometimes, our customers even adopted the CBRM process and set up their own standard templates, which they then provided to their other key suppliers.

While CBRM can be used as an "us reporting to them" tool, we found it is most beneficial when all sides are contributing relevant information and KPIs, thereby creating a two-way function.

Introduce a key account management strategy cautiously; identifying too many key accounts, with their higher service levels, risks a business's ability to keep its promises. Instead, ensure sufficient time is spent on creating clear differentiation between each band and stick to that definition.

It is much easier to start small and add accounts as the program progresses, as opposed to trying to demote customers once they are aware they are key accounts (Ryals 2012, 2).

Overall, I found the CBRMs were a powerful tool that both customer and supplier committed to. As such, there was always a joint desire and openness to the engagements. Of course, there were also moments when we would have preferred to bury any bad news contained in the shared reports. However, the strong relationships we fostered always allowed us to handle even the most difficult discussions in a more positive and fruitful manner.

Field Service

While not all organizations will have a field service team, they can be a powerful asset where they exist. However, the field service team can suffer from the same, and if not a worse, branding that gets applied to the customer service team.

People often view them negatively, referring to them as "just mobile engineers with a toolbox" or "only ever needed when something has gone wrong." I respectfully disagree, and the following points show this team's value.

- A question for you to consider. Who in your business has the most in-depth understanding of both how your products and services operate in the field and the customer challenges associated with them?

  I can tell you that most of the time it will not be design engineers, or manufacturing engineers, or anyone from the OEM—instead, it will be your field service team. So, who better to take an integral role within your sales activities (and those of new OEM product design)?

  This application of lateral thinking can provide a simple-to-implement, but potentially powerful, addition to your sales (and design) efforts. However, I can also tell you that this is an often-overlooked benefit (also see Warranty).

- Apart from demonstrating your clear commitment to supporting your products, field service engineers could spend a considerable amount of time with your customers. Therefore, along with the sales team, they are the mobile external face of your business. Effectively, they are your technical eyes and ears on the ground in the marketplace.

- Their audience within your customer base is likely to differ from who your sales team interacts with. This presents an opportunity to reinforce regular positive messaging about your business within another area of your customers' organization.

- The field service team's discussion of product performance and operations can, by extension, result in the customers' technical staff influencing the buying decisions of their purchasing team.

- Engineers talk in a binary fashion, so facts—ones and zeros—and not in the endless commercial and sales "tap dancing" that accompanies the usual supplier–customer relationship.

We found the technical discussion approach to be very beneficial. Many times, it helped us to open doors, uncover vital information, enhance our proposals, and overcome challenges with our customers' purchasing and commercial personnel.

- Your technical teams will also discuss the performance of your products and possibly similar and/or co-located items from other suppliers, gathering vital competitive intelligence.

  Your staff having routine discussions with your customers about product performance and issues they face means they are in a great position to spot new opportunities.

  Such active intelligence gathering can, therefore, provide new opportunities for RMU and service projects, adding further strength to your value propositions and commercial offerings.

- Sometimes, the field service team will resort to their tools and implement in-field fixes, thereby reducing operational disruption for your customers.

  Similarly, they can also implement in-field fixes on products that would otherwise need returning for warranty repair, thereby alleviating significantly higher internal-processing and handling costs for your business.

- Offering regular technical reviews to your customers is an extra service that can transform field service from a reactive team to proactive problem-solvers, setting you apart from your competitors.

- Another great use for an often-underutilized resource relates to training. No one is better placed than the field service team to understand your customers' knowledge limitations and challenges regarding the use of your product and services.

  As a result, they are in the ideal position to identify potential training needs that could generate new value for your customers and revenue for your business.

Finally, here is a great example of how a difficult situation drove some radical thinking, which resulted in another positive outcome for this team.

The inevitable difficult downturns in the economy create their own challenges. Typically, the first outcome is a need for staff reduction. It was only after experiencing this that I realized customer-facing teams needed a clearer business value whenever workable. Therefore, we started looking at ways for the field service team to generate revenue from its activities.

One solution allowed our customers to reduce the level of unscheduled equipment failures and subsequent disruption to their business. Our field service team achieved this by developing a new program of chargeable product health checks. These took place at the customer's place of business and negated the need for a significant amount of equipment being removed and returned unnecessarily.

This may appear counterintuitive to generating MRO sales, but it was not. The low level of repair required on these unnecessary returns did not allow for normal MRO pricing and margins to apply, and so, effectively, they were clogging up our shopfloor with low-value work.

In effect, the customer goodwill and loyalty generated by this program far outweighed the loss of low-value MRO. Within 18 months of the project start, the field service department had become self-funding, and, within two years, it was turning a profit on its activities.

Technical Support

Some organizations view technical support and field service as allied services, and they assign one team to perform both roles. I have always worked with two separate teams, but I firmly believe that regardless of the setup, both teams are equally important and valuable assets. Here are some reasons:

- The first point is to emphasize the importance of committing to the technical support process when providing a product or service. This will significantly affect your customer's perception of your business.

- The technical support team will also be in routine daily contact with your customers. As per the field service team, their audience is also likely to be a different set of contacts to your other customer-facing teams.

    Once again, the potential for gathering valuable customer and competitor intelligence through the daily customer contact conducted by your outward-facing personnel is unmatched by any other source.

- Technical support teams within an MRO business are typically office based, and so they are likely to see a significantly larger element of your customers' products and queries first hand compared to a field service team. As such, they will develop a very strong understanding of your products, performance, and particularly the reliability. Therefore, if you have technical products and services that you routinely modify, enhance, and/or upgrade, they are in an ideal position to be an integral part of those discussions with your customer.

So, with your customer-facing teams, it is all about recognizing that these are not necessarily the limited functions that your organization may have considered them to be. Instead, it is crucial to explore their full potential and, therefore, maximize the ROI.

Finally, it is worth talking about how you set up these teams, as there are many approaches. I have heard some say that "These are all separate functions that need to be kept apart" and "engineers need quiet" and so on. Others have said that to have multirole teams with customer service staff owning the administrative relationship, that is, warranty, pricing, and service, is open to conflicts of interest or abuse.

Of course, with financials, such as pricing and warranty, it is important to have proper processes, sign-offs, and oversight controls in place to prevent such issues. However, once those protections are in place, a coordinated team with a comprehensive understanding of the customer is the ideal environment for decision-making.

Ultimately, the aim is to cultivate a cohesive "Account Team" that possesses a comprehensive understanding of every aspect of a customer's relationship with your business.

By working together, they can achieve the perfect balance between delivery and responsiveness, as illustrated in Figure 5.1.

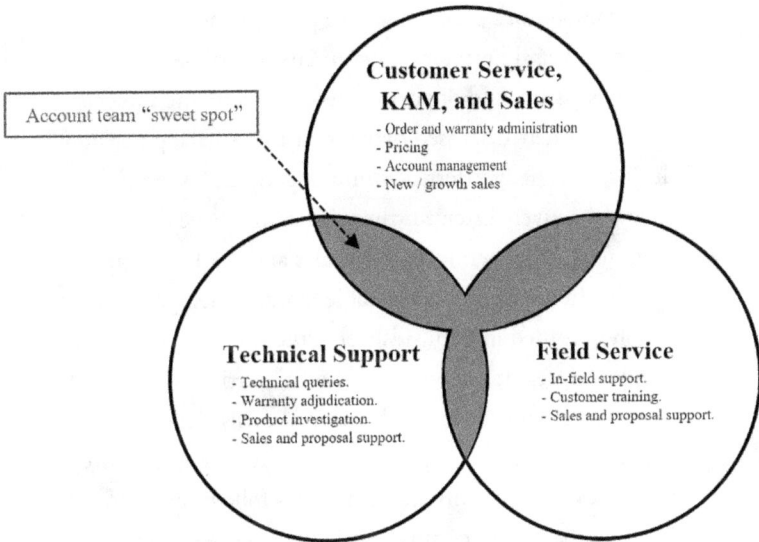

Figure 5.1 The service "sweet spot" of core after-sales day-to-day functions

I acknowledge that all organizations have their unique characteristics, and thus variance to the neat three-team structure shown here is quite possible. However, the goal remains the same, and that is to have all customer-facing personnel working together cohesively. This will enable a direct hit on the after-sales service "sweet spot."

Top Tips

- Some perceive the customer service teams as passive in their role, but that is wasting a potentially great resource. Instead, consider having them actively pursue opportunities for your business by leveraging their customer relationships and the frequent communication they facilitate.
- Achieving the service sweet spot discussed above is best achieved by having all the customer-facing teams working within the same reporting structure. This approach mitigates

the risk of inconsistencies in management, messaging, and purpose.

- Market data-mining can reveal critical information on both your competitor's product/service performance issues and selling activity and keep tabs on your customers' needs.

  These issues and opportunities are exactly the subjects being routinely discussed by your customer-facing personnel during their daily external communications. So, train them to seek and actively listen for these issues and have them record them for further action by your sales and marketing personnel.

  This freely accessible, valuable market intelligence can be simply recorded in a spreadsheet, although my recommendation is to integrate a dedicated "Leads" section within a CRM. This central information hub ensures consistent data storage that will serve as the single source of truth for your entire organization and support all formal sales follow-up.

- Some of the best sales opportunities I have seen started life as simple leads generated by the customer service team. So, it pays to never underestimate the value that the services team can deliver to your business if used correctly.

Warranty Support

A warranty should not be viewed as just a cost to a business, instead it is an investment in customer loyalty. But this is often an area of business that is given little attention or coverage, and yet it remains one of the most contentious influences on customer relationships.

It is an area that can cost a business very significant sums of money through correcting poor design and/or quality and lack of proactive feedback to enable quick, effective remedial/preventative action. There are other considerations, such as customer dissatisfaction and avoidable incurred costs through poor warranty administration.

Many customers opt to claim warranty on a high percentage of items and delegate the management to their suppliers because of either an inability or unwillingness to handle it internally within their organizations.

Another type of customer is those who recognize their supplier's incompetence in handling warranties and intentionally submit false claims to exploit this weakness and gain an advantage.

Having identified that warranty can be a substantial risk, just where do suppliers commonly get their approach to its management wrong?

The first key mistake is to view warranty as a commercial function and have it solely administered by nontechnical personnel.

In fact, the commercial warranty decision is the simplest—essentially being a binary or simple "yes/no" decision typically based on time elapsed, be that calendar or usage based.

It is the technical decision where the complexity lays. It needs to determine not only the actual cause of the failure but also whether that falls within the scope of the applicable contractual terms. Administering this technical analysis against a previous repair becomes more challenging, as any warranty usually applies specifically to the area of the last repair.

So, the actual warranty adjudication should normally comprise a two-step process—step (1) being an initial decision on whether the claim qualifies commercially, based on the elapsed time analysis. If the claim passes step (1), it advances to step (2), where technical experts examine the cause of failure and assign liability accordingly.

Regardless of whether a claim is accepted or rejected, it is best practice to communicate the decision to the customer immediately, fully explaining the reasons for any rejection.

You will need to evaluate who in your organization is most suitable for the technical adjudication process.

As an example, we utilized our field service team along with the factory-based technical support team. It was undeniable that they had the greatest understanding of the products and their performance within the customer base compared to anyone else in the organization.

This larger pool of combined resource and experience proved very effective, and significant technical disputes over warranty decisions became a thing of the past.

As the field service team was directly involved in the warranty adjudications, they could also act as a feedback conduit, providing our customers with concise information about their repairs.

This feedback service provided guidance on reducing the usual causes for technical rejection of warranty claims. These included customer-induced damage, incorrect handling and operation, as well as unnecessary removals. For example, it addressed cases where customers mistakenly removed a product believing it to be faulty, despite it being fully operational.

Ultimately, this service became a firm favorite of our customers and a best practice *unique selling point (USP)* of our after-sales offering.

Warranty terms are usually a legally binding principle, but some organizations may stretch the boundaries by rejecting valid claims, especially when there is sales and margin pressure caused by external economic factors. But a warranty is a promise, and a promise kept builds trust.

Given that this is such a contentious area in supplier–customer relationships, it is hard to understand why anyone would risk damaging that trust and face legal challenges when their position is unjustified. To me, this is a "lose-lose" scenario and not one that any business trying to be a top performer should indulge in.

Another aspect of warranty is where an organization may conduct MRO activities under the license (approval) of a third party (such as an OEM). Effectively, the licensee repairs products for its customers under the OEM's warranty terms.

I once worked for an organization that used to perform warranty repairs for its customers under just such an agreement.

After completing the repairs, we would claim back the appropriate labor and material costs from that third party.

I was running after-sales product support, and we were driving the team to spend significantly more time out with our customers. However, we were being met with high levels of customer dissatisfaction related to our warranty decisions.

At that time, the commercial department was running the warranty process with limited technical input. As previously noted, insufficient product knowledge compromised accurate decision making, leading to avoidable customer dissatisfaction.

Following considerable effort by the technical team, facilitated by the support of senior management, warranty management responsibilities were subsequently transferred to the former.

Within 18 months, we had completely restructured the process and streamlined the activity on the shopfloor. This had reduced incurred warranty repair delays, significantly improved customer satisfaction, and increased the available technical department resources through reduced wasted effort. Moreover, the improved administration accomplished the following:

- A reduction in the number of our material and labor reimbursement claims being rejected by the OEM.
- A reduction in the number of customer warranty claims being incorrectly accepted.

All this activity delivered the company an effective increase in revenue of approx. $1.5M p.a. and just goes to show what a little focus can achieve.

We also recognized a problem existed with the new product design coming from our own OEM parent. This situation was not being helped by a distinct and unhelpful gulf between their design and our after-sales technical teams.

This prompted us to redesign the process that ensured we recorded the warranty costs incurred against each of the products. Further analysis confirmed that new products were showing a worrying similarity to the reliability issues and failure trends of their forerunners.

This information became the basis of scheduled monthly "warranty cost driver" reviews, which provided us with early warnings of quality and/or design issues.

Importantly, this simple data collection activity allowed us to accurately assign tangible and potentially avoidable cost data. Previously, warranty cost had been regarded as an intangible, peripheral cost of doing business. But the combining of technical and financial information brought a much greater focus to the subject.

Following an internal review among the after-sales technical community, we also identified several potential improvement ideas that were later proposed to the OEM engineering director. After discussion, we agreed to implement a concurrent design approach:

- A regular new product reliability and warranty cost report being formally distributed to the engineering team.
- The OEM design engineers would serve a "tour of duty" as part of their formal vocational training. This involved spending time within the after-sales repair shop, sitting alongside our shopfloor tradespeople as they assessed and fixed our customers' products.
- Regular product review meetings between the after-sales field service and technical support teams and the OEM design team were instigated and formalized.
- The OEM design team accompanied the after-sales team on in-field visits so that they could both discuss issues directly with the customer and see the products in situ.

The concurrent design project had many significant benefits, including:

- Enhancement of new product design.
- Shorter lead times to implement reliability improvements.
- A closer working relationship between the design and after-sales teams.
- The design team felt better-connected to their products as they were more familiar with the real-life operational conditions as opposed to them being drawing board–based concepts.
- After-sales shopfloor repair personnel gained more job satisfaction, as they felt they could now positively

influence the new designs with their extensive product knowledge.

- Finally, and most importantly, reduced overall warranty cost and improved customer satisfaction.

Later, the engineering director acknowledged that the project had a major positive impact on product design, adding that, in retrospect, earlier implementation would have been preferable.

Having now successfully applied this approach several times, if a business has both new product design and after-sales services, this type of closed feedback loop is best practice.

In MRO, where there is a warranty dispute, there is usually also an unpaid and disputed invoice. Cash flow is king in any business. Having delays in the order-to-cash cycle caused by either poor management within the process or, at worst, spurious adjudications is a self-inflicted wound.

Of course, it also goes without saying that each correctly rejected warranty claim is another product/service that can be charged for and is, therefore, an additional revenue-generating sale.

While leading the support function in various organizations, a regular topic of customer complaint included the perennial nugget—"You reject an unacceptably high proportion of our warranty claims."

To counter this, we instigated a very simple fix that involved the application of a final decision code against each customer claim submitted. From that data, we could produce standardized warranty results for each customer that showed exactly how the decisions on their claims broke down. In 99 percent of cases, having this information readily available was more than sufficient to kill the complaints.

In fact, we went one stage further and included it within "Monthly Performance Reports" for our key customers (see CBRM). This approach effectively managed and addressed any potential negative narrative about warranty.

From the previous discussion, it is clear the effective management of the warranty process within any organization should be a basic requirement, with a high potential for reward.

In addition, it also has value as a marketing tool, as administering and controlling it effectively allows for its use as part of the customer satisfaction suite of tools. Here are two good examples of this:

> You may already have personal or business experience of the frustration caused by having a claim rejected because something failed just outside of its warranty period.
>
> However, it is now common for many suppliers to have rewards schemes for their biggest and most strategic customers—anything from points that convert to cash, to free upgrades, and so on.
>
> The same process can apply to warranty adjudication. A good example would be to grant key customers more flexibility on the time/calendar terms of their claims. In such instances, the company can extend the consideration as a "goodwill gesture without precedent" against a specific claim(s).
>
> Formally notifying the customer that you have granted a concession also ensures they are aware and that your positive action does not just slip under the radar.
>
> The second example relates to the length of warranty periods (particularly related to repairs) and how they can be a key differentiator in sales bids.
>
> To take advantage of this potential benefit, you will need to have a strong understanding of your product reliability and warranty administration data. Said data will allow you to perform the necessary detailed financial risk/impact analysis associated with any potential fixed extension of the terms.

In summary, organizations often overlook and downplay the importance of the warranty function—but running it effectively and efficiently can deliver significant benefits:

- Improved customer satisfaction and reduced customer disputes.
- Reduced reputational damage.
- Increased sales and reduced warranty costs.
- No unnecessary legal action and associated costs.

- Improved order-to-cash cycle time.
- Enhanced product/service design.
- Additional USPs for sales and marketing.
- Additional data to counteract customer negativity/complaint and to support customer account management.

Top Tips

- As a minimum, best practice is to always ensure that you apply the warranty terms your customers are legally entitled to. Then use additional "considerations" as part of your marketing tools to enhance customer satisfaction and relationships as appropriate.

Special Tools and Test Equipment

As part of their obligations as an OEM, many are duty-bound to produce technical-servicing data for their merchandise.

Such data are usually in the form of a document, commonly referred to as repair, overhaul, component maintenance, and/or servicing manual. These manuals provide detailed instructions for servicing and maintaining specific products. OEMs with broad product ranges may have hundreds of such documents in their portfolio.

As with any servicing activities, general engineering tooling you might find in any local garage will be required, but there may also be a need for *specialist tooling and test equipment (STTE)*.

The technical data related to STTE is also the IP or "secret sauce" of an OEM business, so the business should nurture and protect it. However, I have encountered organizations that possess many manuals that include substantial amounts of STTE but lack a formal process for controlling these products related to their manufacture, management, and distribution.

In fact, at least two companies I know of found it "Too difficult to manage STTE." Whenever they received a customer request, they would simply send the technical data (free of charge), as it was the easiest solution. This is a dereliction of duty, as it neglects the organization's best interests for the sake of convenience.

Besides a business losing its "secret sauce," there are a few other impacts of such a strategy:

- Loss of revenue from making and selling STTE.
- Increased competition and loss of MRO sales (as competitors have easy access to critical data and lower startup costs).
- Loss of licensing and maintenance revenue relating to the sale and ongoing upkeep of STTE.

Put simply, better management and control of IP, including STTE, by an organization will result in increased revenue year over year and an extended after-sales longevity.

Top Tips

- If your business has STTE associated with it, ensure that you fully evaluate its potential commercial value. Where appropriate, build the required structure (processes, controls, resources) to extract the full value from it.

Maintenance, Repair, Overhaul, and Spares

Earlier, I discussed how controlling IP is important and should not be underestimated in terms of after-sales revenue streams. So, defining the strategy for products that require ongoing MRO (and therefore spares) is critical, as these products may require repeated servicing over many years.

The sale of *spares* is usually more attractive than MRO to an OEM because of the higher markup (profit margin) and no significant additional transaction costs. However, OEM after-sales that are focused purely on spares sales can lead to unintended consequences in the future, such as:

- How can an organization effectively manage its reputation if it is outsourcing the MRO process to third parties who may significantly impair customer perceptions of product reliability and performance?

- How will an OEM analyze and critique warranty cost reimbursement claims received from their approved third-party sources if they have no or limited in-house experience with the product? Conducting MRO provides a hands-on level of detailed knowledge that is very difficult to get at arm's length. Such knowledge is vital to achieving reliable, fact-based cause of failure decisions, that is, defining whether it was a product design or quality issue, an MRO workmanship issue, or an issue caused by the customer.
- How can an organization design the next generation of products if it does not have firsthand data on both the use of its products and the technical findings from any subsequent servicing process?
- If third parties control the product MRO, how are the data required to deploy rapid product redesign and prevent high warranty costs and/or product performance penalties, accessed?
- How is IP leakage controlled, as a divested MRO strategy would require an OEM to provide active support and technical information to third parties?
- How can the demand for spares and repairs be maintained and protected if third parties control the MRO decision-making?

  While a third-party license can help protect an OEM's supply chain, independent organizations will naturally want to make their own decisions where they source their spares from. They could utilize alternate parts, USM, locally developed repair schemes and MRO *smart scoping* to minimize part replacements and, therefore, purchase of spares from the OEM.

Several OEMs that I have worked with have fallen foul of exactly the above points with a subsequent negative impact on their long-term after-sales costs and sales.

Alternatively, while an OEM can elect to be heavily MRO focused and deploy significantly stronger control of its IP, this approach also has its own drawbacks:

- Exclusivity: Customers will probably view any attempt to control a high percentage of the MRO as anticompetitive. Customers

like to have a choice and not just because that can mean reduced
market pricing.

- Choice/Competition: Customer pressure for a choice of supplier
  and convenience (are you located conveniently?).
- Lost Margin: MRO can have a lower margin than spares sales, as
  OEM after-sales try to undercut the pricing of their independent
  competitors.
- Price Pressure: It may be hard to maintain a true OEM-type
  MRO approach, that is, without the usual cost options that an
  independent supplier can provide. Why is this the case? Well,
  often OEMs prioritize quality and "maintaining their standards"
  (also known as "gold plating"), which can lead to higher MRO
  pricing when compared to independent suppliers.

From my standpoint, the best way forward (if you are an OEM) lies
somewhere between the two extremes (total spares vs. total MRO focus)
outlined above. Therefore, the support journey begins with a decision on
how much of the MRO/spares market you want to keep.

Whatever you choose to do, you will need to assess the impact of all
the above points and consider appropriate mitigating actions.

If you are an independent MRO purchasing spares from an OEM,
then you may well be paying a higher price than what they charge for
those parts within their own services. As a result, you are likely to have
two options that need to be considered.

Becoming an affiliated supplier has benefits, such as purchasing discounts, but it may also come with restrictions. For example, these restrictions can limit your ability to offer anything other than OEM-level
service and spares. However, a closer working relationship, technical support, and discounts from the OEM are also not insignificant benefits.

Alternatively, if you remain truly independent, you have significantly
more freedom to act in your own best interests.

All of these are viable options, and it really comes down to your preferred strategy and any commercial terms you can agree.

Certainly, staying independent allows far more control—for example, the use of USM and reuse of worn parts (that have no impact
on the product integrity/ reliability). Additionally, the introduction of

repair schemes to reduce the number of parts that actively need replacing with new.

Another option is to customize your spare parts purchases from OEMs to coincide with discount periods, such as the end of financial periods (quarter, half year, and year).

Of course, you can always try to adopt a hybrid role that sits somewhere between the extremes.

Begin by conducting a strategy review and analyzing the various options (see Business Modeling) to decide where you would like to sit.

I have worked extensively in businesses with complex engineered products. A common denominator has always been the weakness of the supply chain between the OEM and their after-sales MRO/distributor division and the negative impact on the latter's performance.

This seems to be an OEM-focused issue, as independent MRO and spares distribution organizations providing services on the same product lines seem to fare much better. I believe the OEM's challenges are down to three main reasons:

1. As previously discussed, they typically prefer high-volume new production runs with a regular scheduled delivery profile planned at their full manufacturing lead times.
2. They rarely like the smaller manufacturing volumes associated with *out of production (OOP)* equipment being supported by their after-sales team.
3. Holding inventory for future events (not covered by firm customer orders) is an anathema to an OEM. As a result, they will often apply similar inventory restrictions on their after-sales division. Unfortunately, these restrictions rarely provide a buffer for their own, often highly variable delivery performance, or reflect the level of after-sales customer demand variance.

If the above were not bad enough, with the OEM controlling the manufacturing, they also essentially control the allocation of the finished products. This power to control the direction of distribution can manifest itself in behaviors that are also particularly damaging to the after-sales MRO and spares delivery performance. For example, in situations of unmet production targets or strained supply chains insufficient to meet both production and after-sales demand, OEMs can strategically allocate resources to satisfy their own needs.

This is not an unusual event, even though the APD clearly benefits the OEM from selling through the after-sales marketplace.

Returning to the independent suppliers—they are 100 percent after-sales focused and, as a result, do not suffer the split-personality issues of many OEMs. Their success depends on their ability to provide high-quality service, so they are more proactive in dealing with the expected challenges that come with complex engineered products. In contrast a typical OEM-owned after-sales response to such challenges is to turn and shout at their manufacturing division at ever-increasing levels of volume and frustration.

It has been established that OEMs are capable of, and do, make decisions with negative consequences for their after-sales divisions. Sometimes, this will be exacerbated by the deployment of restrictions that prevent the latter from seeking solutions routinely deployed by the independent organizations they are competing against.

As an example, one after-sales organization I have experience with had a lamentable delivery performance of spares from their own OEM production division (<50 percent delivery on time).

This situation had been going on for years, and they had tried the usual pleading and threatening. They had also endured countless "improvement projects," all without significant and/or sustainable improvement.

The following points are included to assist with the context of this example:

- The after-sales division was owned and fully controlled by the OEM, as opposed to them having true independence of decision-making.
- The after-sales team faced pressure from both customers and, interestingly, the OEM board itself, because of the poor customer performance metrics. They were also put

under intense pressure to deliver sales growth, despite the OEM's delivery performance directly and significantly impairing their ability to improve on either issue.

Being aware that independent providers regularly outperformed them in meeting customer needs, the after-sales team investigated their competitors' supply chain models for a solution. Essentially, there were two key tactics being utilized:

1. Holding significantly higher inventories (at risk) to smooth the peaks and troughs of spares deliveries caused by OEM manufacturing and delivery issues.
2. To address delivery delays or shortages, they secured spares from other independent MRO and distributor organizations worldwide.

When presented with both the above strategies as potential solutions to the delivery challenges, the OEM rejected them and prohibited the implementation of either.

The decision to reject point (1) was based on the expected escalation of inventory-holding costs, which would have negatively impacted the company's financial status.

The reason for rejecting point (2) was that it would have led to a decrease in demand for the manufacturing division and a reduction in the after-sales operating margin. This is because the latter would have had to pay higher (open market) spares prices for their critical parts as opposed to receiving them at an intercompany-transfer price from the OEM.

As a last resort, a potential third option was explored. This involved manufacturing the critical after-sales spares requirements (specifically those the OEM were failing to deliver on time) through a third-party organization solely dedicated to addressing those needs.

This would have removed the constant noise of critical demand from the OEM and provided after-sales with a solution with significantly more flexibility and ability to react.

Once again, the board dismissed the suggestion as too expensive, adding the loss of IP control to their previous concerns about cost and lower demand for their manufacturing division.

So, in this example, you have the OEM:

- Pressurizing the after-sales team to improve both their delivery performance and sales growth, with both being negatively affected by the actions of the OEM.
- Failing to resolve the issues and, in fact, wanting to keep sole manufacturing control, despite being unable to deliver products on time and sustainably.
- Preventing the after-sales team from implementing proven solutions.

If you had not actually experienced this for yourself, you could be forgiven for thinking that I had made it up. But I can assure you it happened, and, unfortunately, it persisted for a considerable period.

Now, I am not suggesting that this type of relationship is typical of all such organizations. In fact, I am sure that there are many after-sales organizations that receive reliable supply performance from their manufacturing division. However, these issues are still prevalent in businesses today, and I am sure many of you can relate to them.

You could rightly ask what the solution to such a conundrum might be. I would say *"many and varied"* (not least because of the variation of operational demands across the multitude of after-sales business segments). Such potential solutions might include any of the following:

- Have the OEM fix their supply chain.
  This is, of course, the obvious and ideal aim, but, in truth, I have yet to see an OEM achieve this sustainably. Instead, they continue to struggle with their own supply chains and the volatility of after-sales demand.
- Granting the after-sales organization full operational and financial decision-making autonomy.
  Let them live and die by their own decision-making.

- Permitting the after-sales team to purchase critical spares from open market/independent distribution sources.
  Why cause customer and reputational harm and potentially incur financial delivery penalties if the spares are available and sitting on a shelf somewhere?
- Any/all after-sales customer performance penalties arising directly from failures in the OEM supply chain to be passed back to and fulfilled by the OEM.
  Financial pain is a great motivator to drive change and improve!
- The OEM recognizing and taking responsibility for their delivery issues.
  This would involve granting the after-sales organization the financial bandwidth necessary to hold additional buffer inventory to smooth out the inconsistent OEM delivery performance.
- Have OOP spares made by 100 percent after-sales–focused manufacturing organizations (either owned or independent). This would remove the demand variability from the OEMs' line of sight, allowing them to concentrate on their current production manufacturing.
  While an independent solution would be the ideal approach, it may not be acceptable. Therefore, another potential option could involve embedding manufacturing lines dedicated to after-sales within the OEM facility. Previous attempts have shown limited success; hence, for this to have any chance of working, it is crucial that any such line(s) have independent management and true capacity separation. However, I would still reserve judgment whether this would be enough for this to work given the obvious challenges that sharing a facility would create.
- Permitting the after-sales team to implement strategies that reduce their demand for spares from the OEM. These might include utilizing USM, implementing repair schemes, and easing inspection requirements for in-service products.

You may be an independent business that works in the same market as the OEMs. If so, one of the best things for you is that OEM organizations face significant supply chain challenges for the many reasons outlined in this book. In fact, I would go as far as to say that even the very best OEM after-sales divisions can still routinely struggle to deliver spares and MRO consistently.

Conversely, independent distributors and MRO organizations acknowledge the necessity of maintaining inventory. They view it as a strategy for differentiating themselves from their competitors. Their actions serve as evidence of their steadfast belief in the often-said truism—"They who have the inventory, have the sale."

In the aerospace industry, independent MRO providers and distributors have seen significant growth. This is largely due to the OEMs' after-sales divisions failing to meet customer needs and/or demand.

Hampered by inappropriate operating systems and all the other reasons already touched on above, this situation is unlikely to change soon, and this is great news for independent organizations.

Some may consider certain aspects mentioned above as heresy. However, those who struggle with the persistent challenge of OEM supply chain performance will undoubtedly comprehend the necessity for a change to unlock the full potential of their after-sales organizations.

Top Tips

- In summary, MRO and spares are central to so many organizations and critical to being able to meet customer requirements, but challenges remain.

  Therefore, my strong recommendation for OEM after-sales organizations is that they must examine closely how the successful independent organizations operate and incorporate their best points.

  In fact, I am convinced they must become more like their independent competitors if they wish to maintain and grow their position.

- For independent organizations, the advice is simply to continue monitoring the activities of both the OEMs and your other competitors for weakness, shortfalls, and gaps to customer needs.

CHAPTER 6

Commercial Activities

Commercial/Contracts

Over the years, I have reviewed and constructed many contracts—be that after-sales sections within OEM contracts or pure after-sales agreements. The formats have been diverse, covering everything from: comprehensive OEM *general terms agreements (GTA)*; and for after-sales, both simple fixed price and complex reliability-based price per hour (usage) agreements.

Therefore, despite my background being technical, I can confidently say that I know my way around a contract. However, having worked in and around many OEM organizations, there has been a depressingly familiar approach to the commercial part of a business. Unfortunately, this is where they show a lack of trust and insist that "Only an OEM-experienced individual can lead the commercial aspects of after-sales."

This is completely misguided and, in fact, a damaging position to take. As I mentioned earlier, the tempo of an OEM and that of an after-sales business are so different that it is challenging for them to work effectively under the same roof. The same applies here. Furthermore, the quantity of both customers and contracts that an OEM has will normally be an order of magnitude lower.

Those simple facts alone mean that while there is variance in OEM contracts, the after-sales customer base generates a much greater contract quantity and variety of terms. So, an individual's mindset, problem-solving ability, and flexibility are very important features of the best after-sales commercial personnel.

Please do not misunderstand my comments here, as there are some brilliant commercial OEM employees, and I have certainly worked alongside some great examples. Yet, while these may exist, I am yet to see one that has been as effective in an after-sales role as the commercial after-sales specialists I have worked with.

Similarly, I have seen after-sales organizations—where dedicated commercial teams exist—insisting that only they are capable of contractual negotiation. At times, this has resulted in the salespeople being completely excluded from the closing of deals.

If you are an organization that is following this path, I would humbly suggest that you do not have the right sales staff. Unfortunately, I have seen this approach result in the following negative outcomes:

- Customer confusion and a loss of the relationship the salesperson will have built during the selling process.
- Despite thorough handover briefings, the commercial team may not have been involved in earlier discussions, leading to unnecessary disconnects between the customer and the supplier.

  That lack of familiarity can mean they are also very unlikely to have the same in-depth understanding of the customer's culture, behaviors, and "temperature" on the many points to be covered.
- Simple misunderstandings in context and approach.
- The opportunity for the customer to use "you said"/"they said" tactics regarding the missing salesperson, to sow doubt and division and weaken a negotiating position.

My recommendation is to either train your sales staff to handle closing discussions or adopt a negotiating team approach that combines the sales team's knowledge with the contractual expertise of your commercial team.

To emphasize this teaming point, while I would class myself as an after-sales expert, I am also very much a generalist with a broad and deep set of experience. But, while I am comfortable with the day-to-day operational workings and implications of a contract, for the specialist sections, for example, legal and insurance, I would rely on a subject-matter expert from within that field.

Whatever final negotiating structure you may conclude is best for your organization, I would strongly emphasize the need to have strong specialist (legal) support for your contracting. Your chosen commercial expert may have the appropriate experience to deliver that support, or it could be additional services from other internal or external sources.

Another area to examine is the style of language used within contracts. When I started my career, many agreements used full legalese and were liberally sprinkled with archaic terms like "hereinbefore," "whereunder," "aforesaid," and so on. This type of "muddy" language caused issues, and we frequently found ourselves in the embarrassing position of trying to clarify it with our customers and struggling to do so.

Similarly, the staff (supplier and customer) who managed the products and services covered by these agreements on a day-to-day basis also found them too complex to understand.

Fortunately, the commercial team leader at the time could also see the general direction of travel and the need for greater simplicity and clarity. After much discussion, we decided to act.

Thereafter, I spent a significant amount of time during my early introduction to the commercial business world, rewriting our contract templates in plain English.

In addition, I have witnessed instances where businesses intentionally use legalese and complex contract construction to obfuscate and mislead or conceal the true intent.

This type of action hardly contributes to the construction and maintenance of good long-term client relations, and I have found that the truth will always find a way out. Once your customers realize that they have been "tricked" into an unfair, or overly restrictive agreement, the response is likely to be very negative.

Customers who find themselves in such circumstances can broadcast this publicly, damaging your prospects with both existing and potential new clients. In the worst cases, the customer can also use a "sales stop" notice, effectively blocking your business from accessing any further orders and/or new growth opportunities.

Top Tips

- Engage all internal stakeholders early in the contractual process to prevent unintended delays and provide opportunity for any potential "red flags" as early as possible.
- If your agreements contain mathematical formulae, or complex interdependent terms, I strongly recommend that you

include worked examples showing how these would act in each relevant scenario. By doing so, you enhance openness and clarity during the initial sales effort and subsequent negotiations.

In addition, you will also simplify the ongoing management for both your own and the customer's staff, who will administer the terms once implemented.

- If you plan to have multiple agreements with the same customer (perhaps across a variety of product and service lines), always try to put a GTA in place first. Having such an agreement will significantly speed up any subsequent negotiations and contracting work.

Request for Proposal/Quotation

I have worked with many RFPs during my career. This includes as a contributor to the construction of such documents for issue to others and as a part of a team required to build a response to a customer.

At the beginning of my career, customer experience and expectations were considerably lower than they are today. Therefore, the RFP was a significantly simpler and less onerous beast to both respond to and, importantly, live with if we were fortunate enough to win the bid.

It is fair to say the complexity and demands have risen exponentially over the years. In fact, some customers have simply taken a "pick and mix" approach to their RFP construction, essentially adopting all the "best" requirements from previous RFPs in the marketplace.

From a supplier's perspective, bid documents built in this manner are a nightmare scenario, as they incorporate some of the most restrictive and penalty-laden terms.

The first question to be asked when most people see an (any) RFP is "how should we handle it?"

Well, first it is worth stressing that these documents and how you respond to them provide a window into your business. This is particularly true if you have no previous history with the issuing customer. Here are some key points:

- First impressions really do count, and so you need to avoid giving a customer any reasons to be negative. This will help to prevent your efforts from falling at the first hurdle.

    Therefore, ensure that you present your responses professionally, with good grammar, no spelling mistakes, and consistent formatting.
- Apply patience and care to fully review and understand each of the customer requirements, both individually and in terms of how they interact and fit into the overall commercial picture.
- It is important to respond to every single line in a customer's RFP. Do not just ignore something because you dislike it or are noncompliant.
- Sometimes, a customer may not have the same first language as you. Alternatively, the person creating the RFP may have a different level of subject understanding.

    Consequently, their document may be confused, or lacking detail and, in such cases, do not hesitate to raise a flag and seek clarification as soon as possible.

    Taking an early approach to such issues will also help to prevent incorrect assumptions and wasted effort in your responses.

Based on my direct experience, I have always used a very simple standard approach to any received RFP. I begin by entering each customer's specifications into a spreadsheet, each on a new row, and identified by the original document number. Then two further columns are added as follows:

Column 1: A simple traffic light color-coding system, assigning a color code to each line as follows:
Red = Noncompliant.
Orange = Partially compliant.
Green = Fully compliant.

Also consider adding a further color, such as blue, to represent those items where your response not only meets the customer's requirement but exceeds it. Proactively highlighting these points ensures the customer does not overlook them.

Column 2: Contains any required explanations/added context for the compliance responses.

Why bother with color-coding? RFPs can easily extend to hundreds of individual line items. So, by adding color, you create three benefits.

The first is that it provides the customer with a quick and clear visual signal of your overall compliance position.

Second, you ensure your bid is benefitting from hitting the right note with those customers with a visual preference when dealing with data.

Third, most organizations strive to create a bid that is compliant and respects their own commercial integrity. However, getting all internal stakeholders on board can sometimes be challenging. So, color-coding provides you and your organization with a quick and easy-to-spot summary of just how compliant your bid is.

Although potentially sobering, this exercise is very useful for both highlighting and focusing attention on those areas where internal stakeholders' responses do not align with bid compliance, especially for strategic or "must win" bids.

Now, sometimes a contrary (or noncompliant) position may be entirely justified. However, from my perspective, this is often not the case. Therefore, a visual representation can be very helpful in refocusing minds on finding a compliant solution.

Some customers may issue their RFPs including traffic light color-coding, which is great, but for those who do not, I would always recommend building it into any response.

Other customers might specify a rigid format of response that does not include a color-based system. In such cases, the recommendation is to follow their instructions 100 percent, but also complete and submit an additional traffic light response as well. I have never had a customer comment negatively on such an additional response.

Once you have completed and submitted your response, try to get an audience with the customer to go through the RFP and pitch your submission in further detail.

Meeting in person can be a valuable opportunity to prevent misunderstandings with a proposal. It also visibly reinforces your commitment to open communication and ensuring that you are meeting the customer's needs.

Some customer organizations operate very strict post-submission RFP/RFQ procedures and do not allow any contact until they make their final decision. In such circumstances, all you can try is some ad hoc/unofficial contact to elicit an update.

In other cases, the customer bid team will be completely open to further discussion, and in those instances, I would recommend scheduling catch-up sessions until they deliver their final decision.

But whatever scenario is in play, your post-bid mantra should be, wherever possible, "follow up, follow up, follow up."

If your business is not focused on long-term contractual arrangements, it is likely that RFQs will play a significant role. In fact, they hold significant importance in some businesses.

Although RFQs are inherently more transactional than RFPs, both present valuable revenue opportunities and sources of business intelligence.

Some businesses show a cavalier disregard toward RFQs; that is, it is a simple binary process of "if we win it's OK" and "if we lose it's OK," with no further consideration or analysis. My experience has shown that even if there is no sale, there is still valuable intelligence available to your business.

As a simple challenge, just ask yourself whether you have accurate, easily accessible data that enables any of the five following points within your business (this equally applies to RFPs):

1. Identification of your "conversion rate," that is, the percentage of RFQs that result in an order versus those that do not, in real time.
2. Analysis and understanding of the reasons why any RFQs did not convert to orders and specifically what the winning competitor had that you did not.

3. Understanding of the products/services that your customers inquire about but you could not provide.
4. Identification of the speed of your RFQ responses (both successful and unsuccessful).
5. Identification of the RFQ conversion rates for the individual members of your sales and/or customer service team.

If you are doing all the above, then great, you have a strong analytical process in operation. If you cannot do any of the above, just consider the potential benefits that you are missing:

1. Day-to-day management of your conversion (win) rate. Setting goals and KPIs for your function and individual team members.
2. Understanding the reasons for both your losses and victories allows you to make data-driven decisions for improvement.
3. Analyzing the orders and products/services you could not supply will provide you with the data you need to build a new opportunity business case. This might include additional stock holdings or improved lead time or new product lines.
4. Perhaps you are operating within a market where speed of response to your customers is critical to achieving successful results. Therefore, being able to analyze your response times when you win versus when you lose could be critical to identifying the need for process improvements and/or additional staff resourcing.

    Being able to both identify these issues and make the changes based on data could enable you to hit the response time "sweet spot," and so raise your win rate.
5. There are many reasons an individual's win rate might be below their colleagues, and these might include: lower levels of experience, training shortfalls, unbalanced workload when compared with their colleagues, and, finally, personal issues.

    If we can identify the win-rate issues early, then we can investigate and proactively deal with the causes.

Finally, it is worth talking about the shape/content of your proposals. As I alluded to earlier, when I started out, the contracts were of an altogether-much-simpler construct. As the market developed, we went through a transitional period that saw us trying to beat our competition by having ever-more-complex offerings. In fact, it almost felt like we were trying to show the customers just how clever we were. This approach, however, presented a significant downside.

The additions frequently failed to benefit the customer, and they often became lost in the labyrinth of increased complexity. Trying to explain our offering was also adding weeks of effort and delay to the sales cycle. Sometimes, we could not even achieve a successful conclusion because of this.

Today, the market has moved on, and, to get ahead of the competition, the aim is to both add value that will truly mean something to the customer and provide more comprehensive solutions.

In B2B, such solutions could very well need to be multilevel to provide all the customer's different stakeholders with positive outcomes for their concerns/issues.

Top Tips

- There may be RFPs/RFQs that you believe are not worth responding to, and, in those cases, you may simply decide to ignore them. However, before doing so, take a moment to consider how that may play out with the customer. Think about how they might react and whether it might affect their future distribution of those requests that you may be interested in.

  Therefore, I would recommend that best practice is to always respond to a customer, even if you are just informing them you will not be submitting a bid (and why).

- Returning to the prime requirement discussed earlier, it is essential to fully understand the customer's needs, problems, and concerns. This will enable you to address as many of these as possible in your proposals.

  For a salesperson, there is nothing more satisfying than when the hard work of the proposal team has enabled them to negate every single concern and question the customer has raised.

Pricing

"Perhaps the reason price is all your customers care about is because you haven't given them anything else to care about," Seth Godin, bestselling author and marketing guru.

Prior to discussing the specifics, it is crucial to acknowledge that pricing is an accurate representation of the perceived value of your service and products to customers.

For any business to be left fighting on price alone in the marketplace is never a healthy prospect. When customers view your products as a commodity that can be purchased anywhere, it generates a lack of loyalty. This can cause a race to the bottom on price, something that will not deliver optimal results consistently.

This is why I believe both the contents of this book and the need for after-sales businesses to deliver excellence are so important.

Service excellence (in its many guises) is a USP and means that your customers are paying for the overall value that you bring to the purchasing decision. The more value you can add, the more you can charge. The words of Ron Johnson, the former chief executive officer of J. C. Penney, echo this: "Pricing is actually a pretty simple and straightforward thing. Customers will not pay literally a penny more than the true value of the product." For example, if you want to be a high-price, high-margin business in a crowded marketplace, a compelling value proposition is essential.

There are many ways to price in after-sales and just how and what strategy (or strategies) you use will depend entirely on the industry/ marketplace you operate in. However, there is no question setting the right product pricing will have significant financial rewards for any organization.

Apart from the obvious benefit of maximizing profits, setting the right prices can also enhance customer satisfaction and loyalty and provide competitive advantage.

The price point and margins you might achieve are dependent on many factors. For instance, after-sales pricing restrictions within formal product support agreements imposed on the OEM by their prime customer may limit your price point and margins.

Or you could be an independent distributor operating under a restrictive agreement with an OEM.

Alternatively, perhaps you are a fully independent business and free to sell your products at whatever price you so wish. Finally, it could be a mix of all these across your catalogue.

Besides contractual restrictions, there are many other factors that affect price, including but not limited to demand and availability, "uniqueness" (level of competition), and development and manufacturing cost. In addition, do not to ignore the customer in the equation, as their needs and expectations are also very important.

There are organizations who deploy dynamic pricing—essentially live flexing of price in response to the day-to-day marketplace. In the B2C world, airlines and hotel chains are a prime example—effectively amending their prices live, dependent on demand and availability.

Some organizations take a simple approach and apply an annual "across the board" price increase to the previous years' catalogue. This may be entirely appropriate if they are working within a highly restrictive pricing environment. However, if that is not the case, I would suggest this is an outdated method and one that will not maximize the financial returns available.

Others using the annual uplift model may attempt to deploy their market knowledge to price each part individually, which is fine when the catalogue is of a manageable size. However, when faced with thousands of products, this can be an administrative nightmare if conducted manually.

I have spent much of my career in an environment where catalogue and/or contractual restrictions largely dominated after-sales pricing.

Changes to prices were typically annual and determined by escalation formulae linked to various formal industry indices. That said, there was always an element that was unrestricted, and, over time, we came to recognize the financial opportunity this presented.

By implementing dynamic pricing on the unrestricted portion of the product range whenever workable, we ensured the extraction of the highest acceptable margin.

Since the items that qualified for dynamic pricing represented a smaller percentage of the overall catalogue, the team managed it manually using a simple price-band method. For example, the pricing flexibility of A band products was very limited because of contractual governance.

The B band comprised those products that were completely unrestricted and so had maximum pricing flexibility. Finally, the C band contained those B band products that were low IP (and therefore easily copied) or that were already subject to competition.

A simple multiplier derived from a contractually stated formulae made it relatively easy to manage the pricing of A band products. The prices of B band products were subject to dynamic amendments based on factors like customers' purchasing history, competitor pricing, and demand and availability.

We also took a similar approach with the C band products, although of course we were always wary of not overdriving the margin. We made further refinements to subdivide the B band products, separating those with the highest IP and/or limited availability.

While the dynamic pricing was a highly successful approach, there was also no question that this manual activity depended on a manageable product range within the relevant band.

The good news is that data analysis and the use of AI can now assist in the deployment of significantly more efficient pricing activity.

Where pricing flexibility exists, AI will also make the dynamic pricing less administratively burdensome by automatically providing recommended pricing based on key data points.

It is interesting that some organizations view after-sales pricing (and specifically spares) as the "gap filler" to be used during the annual sales budget construction process. Unfortunately, this can also lead to high annual price escalation being applied (to fill any sales gap). Worse still, I have seen this happen even when the relevant statistical indices supported much lower values.

However, be aware of the monster you create. Years of high increases will have a compound effect, further separating price from cost, and then the fairness rule will bite.

I believe that "fairness" plays a key role in pricing, as once customers feel that you have ventured into "unjustified" (or "gouging") territory, you will find yourself in troubled water. This will mean those customers who do not find your product a "must have" can walk away.

Furthermore, the wider the cost-versus-price gap is, the more attractive your sales space will become to your competitors.

COMMERCIAL ACTIVITIES   115

This is an issue that the aerospace market has repeatedly witnessed, with OEMs applying "overheated" escalation year over year.

This has continued until the point at which the marketplace has reacted via the increased use of *parts manufacturer approval (PMA)*, independent approved repair schemes, USM, and smart scoping during the MRO process. All these actions depress OEM after-sales spares demand and can cause significant impairment to OEM revenue streams.

It is also common for organizations to employ price reductions as a strategy to increase sales and hit their targets at their key financial reporting points, that is, on a quarterly and annual basis. However, customers can become astute in identifying this pattern, and I have seen many adapt their inventory planning to only make purchases during these periods of price reduction.

Whatever final pricing strategy you decide to adopt, always keep a watch on the bigger picture and ensure that you do not allow it to run out of control.

Top Tips

- There will always be a place for the maximization of sales margin via dynamic pricing. This opportunistic approach to pricing leverages supply and demand pressure and "uniqueness" and can allow a supplier to respond to requests with a significantly higher "spot" price.

  Nevertheless, it is crucial to think carefully and ensure that controls are in place to prevent it from appearing predatory and/or unjustified to the customer. It does not take customers long to realize which suppliers are "gouging" them in their moment of need.

- Make sure not to overlook the customer and any special requests they may have as an area where additional charges can be applied. For example, requests for urgent and expedited order processing or specialized shipping could have additional fees levied.

  The benefit of such fees to a supplier is that they can also fall outside of any contractually restricted pricing that may be in place.

Negotiation

We will start this chapter with a brief discussion of what has been one of my pet hates over many years.

Organizations want their negotiators to secure the most advantageous terms, and yet, one of my most frequently witnessed issues leading to unsatisfactory results relates to travel.

Anyone who has taken a long-haul flight will recognize the potential for brain fog immediately after the journey. The same issue relates to hotel accommodation, which needs to be both comfortable and providing of a good night's rest.

But many organizations apply old-fashioned, hierarchical rules to their staff travel bands. Often this sees key sales and contract negotiating staff travelling in economy, staying in cheap hotels, and making the trips unnecessarily short. This can frequently lead to important negotiations taking place either early the next morning, or worse still, on the day of arrival. Too often for comfort, I have experienced colleagues (and I include myself in this) either too fatigued to follow the discussion intricacies or struggling to stay awake.

Sales and contract negotiations are critical to business success, so why handicap employees and jeopardize those negotiations from the start?

This is a "penny wise, pound-foolish strategy." Karsaklian (2019, 31) supports this view, rightly stating that business travel is an investment in future sales, not a waste of money.

Think, too, about the impact on the employees. You will send them across the globe to negotiate lucrative, strategically important deals, yet you will not provide the support they need to succeed. Now imagine how much more effective their contributions to your business might be if you showed them the respect they deserve and ensured they were always fully prepared.

Of course, I understand that long-haul business class flight prices are significantly higher than economy, but there are also options to mitigate.

- Consider mid-class (premium economy) fares as they still provide a more comfortable seating arrangement.

- Arrange for any negotiations or important meetings to begin at least 24 hours after arrival to allow for rest and recuperation to take place.
- Review the travel policy and amend to provide greater flexibility when important and strategic deals are concerned.

If you cannot implement these options, then I would respectfully suggest that perhaps you have the wrong seniority staff conducting such important meetings.

Having dealt with the housekeeping, let me now clarify the actions that must occur even before meeting the client for negotiations; thorough preparation, including negotiator selection, and both the identification of a strategy and the boundaries within which the discussions and agreement must remain.

One of the key reasons for having a negotiating strategy prepared in advance is that you must always be very mindful that any concessions you grant. As Hughes and Ertel (2020, 7) point out, it can be very difficult to row back from the precedent set by previous concessions and so what gets granted today can set "anchors" for tomorrow's negotiations. In fact, that timeline can be both short and long, as I have even seen early concessions set precedents for customer demands later in the same talks.

In particularly "bullish" organizations, I have seen supplier teams entering negotiations with the express intention of winning on every key point with no thought of compromise. While this can be a directional aim, it should never be a "red line" requirement.

This focus on "beating" the customer as opposed to "winning" the deal is both an unhealthy and self-centered approach to a challenge where the first and most important rule is that you must understand the negotiation is not about you. To move someone from their starting position and reach a point that is acceptable to both parties, intense listening skills are required.

To build trust, you must make the other person feel seen, heard, and understood. By doing so, you can incrementally manage expectations and identify and meet the customer's key needs (Walker 2024, 3).

The next and somewhat obvious point is that it takes two to negotiate, and, for a negotiation to be viewed as a success, there must be "wins" for both sides. Any order or contract won (be that transactional or a short-/long-term agreement) where one side feels hard done by or slighted is not an agreement built on mutual trust. Sure, one can win a long-term deal in such circumstances, but it can also lead to the supplier-facing years of simmering resentment.

This can lead to far higher management costs in the form of complaints, disputes, and challenges as the customer resentment manifests itself in negative behaviors.

Similarly, if it pertains to a transactional order, the supplier might face difficulty in securing future orders. This could lead to increased sales activity costs and, ultimately, lost sales opportunities.

To summarize, because flawlessly favourable negotiations are improbable, a win-win solution necessitates compromise and adaptability from both the customer and supplier. Predetermined *going in (GI)* and *best and final offer (BAFO)* positions are supplier essentials because they define and clarify the potential negotiation range before any discussions occur. Ultimately, to achieve a truly successful conclusion, both sides will need to feel comfortable and satisfied.

Having identified that compromise is the key to a successful long-term contracting arrangement, there are several key observations regarding the negotiation process that I would like to share:

Resourcing

Ensure that you have the right staff for your negotiating team based on the type of bid you are pursuing. As Karsaklian (2019, 31) points out, this includes selecting your negotiator(s) with due consideration to the context and cultural issues they will encounter. For example, do not send someone overseas if they dislike foreign travel, or if they are highly ethnocentric.

For strategic "must win" bids, respect the adage that "two (or more) minds are better than one." Based on personal experience, I can confidently say that using single negotiators on complex bids has generally resulted in suboptimal outcomes.

It is also worth highlighting the use of a negotiating "team" is not an infrequent tactic deployed by customers. In such circumstances, it is virtually impossible for one individual to listen, observe body language, interpret tactics and remain vigilant for potential traps set by the team on the opposite side of the table. Since this can be a daunting challenge, always check in advance with your customer to determine their negotiating team and then set up yours accordingly.

Be mindful though, as regardless of your preparation, there is always the potential for the customer to spring a nasty surprise and not do what they said. Therefore, as a matter of routine, I would never recommend having a single negotiator on a key/strategic bid.

Trench Warfare

Do not let the negotiation get bogged down fighting over any individual clause. I have witnessed far too many deals fail because the negotiating team became fixated on a specific point and neither side would relent.

In such instances, the participants reach an impasse, and, without making progress, the discussions ultimately fail.

When faced with such sticking points, agree to park each issue early and return to it later. The simple act of allowing discussions (and ultimately the relationship between the opposing teams) to flow and mature smoothly can be very beneficial.

Using this strategy, I have successfully resolved many contentious points in an expedient and agreeable manner.

Counting the Concessions

It is important to note that a supplier should not simply give in on every issue the customer may raise, as it sets precedents and will not deliver a successful win-win outcome in the long run.

So, another tip is to record every contentious point that is conceded. These are clear signs of positive intent and evidence of willingness to seek a deal. This information then provides a moral high ground from which to influence the customer's decisions on those key points the supplier needs to secure.

This is another very simple and much-used solution that comes highly recommended.

Insurmountable Barriers

Sometimes, despite all the best efforts, you will become stuck on a seemingly intractable point. The customer may even seem to act in a bloody-minded and/or inexplicable manner.

This occurs more often than you may think and, frequently, can be down to a simple misunderstanding (either theirs or yours), or even direct instruction from their senior management.

I would always recommend taking time out to have "a walk in their shoes" as that different perspective can be enormously helpful in finding a quick solution. If that does not work, then my fallback position is to call a halt to the clash of heads and have an honest discussion. The simple act of having both sides openly discuss their concerns can be enough to resolve many issues.

Despite their simplicity, these techniques have proven to be very effective. I have frequently observed the act of taking a moment to allow a deep breath and step back during tough negotiations can help both parties to gain a clearer understanding of the larger perspective.

When dealing with tough issues, such as a customer's insistence on significant concessions, there is often a temptation to hand over the decision-making responsibility to a higher authority in the organization. Sometimes, this can be the correct thing to do, such as where the authority for that decision does not actually lay with the negotiating team.

However, beware the circumstance where calling senior management into the negotiation is deemed to be the solution.

While this can be successful if the negotiating team has agreed on a clear strategy (and maintains it), senior management may have a desire to be seen as the savior. This can often see them resorting to wearing the proverbial shiny armor and cape in "white knight to the rescue fashion." This behavior can lead to painful decisions, and I have witnessed hard-fought (and justified) negotiating positions collapse when senior management gets involved.

So, if you cannot preplan and agree on a clear strategic negotiation path with the senior(s), including any absolute red lines, it is not advisable to involve them.

To be fair to upper management, it can also be very difficult if the negotiating team simply presents them with the same arguments without providing any additional resolution options.

With no new solutions, this only traps them in the same corner. So, if you choose to follow this path, just be aware that the pressure of trying to create spur-of-the-moment answers during negotiations usually only ever delivers suboptimal outcomes.

Some organizations might have a VBAFO (very best and final offer) position held in the background, just in case their senior management gets involved at some point.

While this can be a successful strategy, be careful as it can also set damaging precedents:

- It undermines the original BAFO position presented by the sales and negotiation team. This can lead to the customer not wanting to negotiate with anyone but senior management in the future.
- It can reset the customer expectations for any future negotiations as they realize that if they push hard enough, there is further value they can extract. Effectively, the customer recognizes that the first BAFO is no longer the real red line for the supplier.
  With both outcomes effectively undermining the resilience of a BAFO position on any current and all future negotiations with a customer, I would recommend:
  - Minimal amendments, and if this is not possible, then present any potential changes as having consequences on the total package being offered. For example, when being challenged on costs, always try to avoid simply cutting prices in response.
- Instead, package and present any reduction as a tradeoff that sees other items being adjusted to a more favorable position.

Once the negotiation is over, and there is a signature on the agreement, the job is done, right? Wrong, you have not closed a deal—you have opened a door to a new cooperation.

The work did not finish with the contract signing, it started there (Karsaklian 2019, ix). Sales and negotiations can take months and involve lots of talking. However, it is really important to never lose sight of the fact the resulting after-sales agreements often run for years and involve lots of action.

Therefore, the aim of such negotiations must be to produce sustainable, deliverable services and support thereafter. Effectively, the winning of the deal is just the first stage in the supplier–client relationship.

However, some suppliers focus so intently on winning a contract they neglect post–contract win requirements. This can lead to the post-win planning taking a backseat and, as a result, poor delivery performance immediately after contract commencement.

I have also witnessed organizations that do not have sufficient control of their operations and processes to enable them to meet either market needs or their contractual obligations. Despite this, they continue to pursue new customer contracts aggressively. These suppliers typically follow one of two paths:

- The "smarter" (some might call them cynical) among them approach this by planning for the inevitable failure and associated penalties by factoring them into their proposal pricing. Effectively, this means the customer is paying an advance levy for the future failures of their supplier.

  However, financial insulation from contractual performance penalties deprives suppliers of a key incentive for improvement. Most times, the old enemy—complacency—sets in, and, without motivation, the supplier does not improve.

- The others are overconfident and adopt a "Don't worry, we'll fix it once we secure the agreement" approach.

  Unfortunately, the supplier can also either overlook the impact of any financial performance penalties or miscalculate and inadequately model their effects.

  There can be immediate negative outcomes, especially if the client involved is large and impactful to the supplier's balance sheet. For instance, drastic cost reductions to fix the finances might worsen problems, especially when the company desperately needs investment to improve performance.

  In situations such as this, a downward spiral may result and that can be extremely difficult to break out of.

> Additionally, knee-jerk cost-cutting measures often ignore the direct costs of managing unhappy customers and the indirect costs of negative publicity.

Either way, the negative impact of public complaints, especially from contracted customers, is significant and rightly raises questions about a company's overall customer support capabilities.

Such feelings in the marketplace will not only dissuade potential ad hoc customers from choosing a supplier but also reduce the prospects of that supplier gaining new contracted customers. This may necessitate a much greater sales effort, revealing another often-underestimated cost.

The pain does not end there as customers who are already unhappy with or are aware of a supplier's poor performance can request heavier performance penalties during subsequent negotiations.

Furthermore, the customers may also demand escape clauses such as delivery performance–related contract termination, or temporary freedom to use other suppliers during any period of nonperformance. A supplier caught in such a position and resisting these demands will simply confirm to the customer that they lack confidence in their own ability to deliver. This raises obvious questions and effectively becomes a "no-win" situation for the supplier.

It is much better to honestly and openly address any known current/potential performance challenges and their solutions during the negotiation.

A straightforward approach fosters customer trust, significantly improving the chances of agreement on contract adjustments before the final signature. These might include either agreeing on a delayed contract start date until solutions are in place or having terms that reflect the performance that is achievable. For example, a customer may demand an order to delivery cycle of 14 days, which the supplier cannot meet from day 1.

In such a case, the draft contract could be amended with a target of 28 days for the first month and 14 days thereafter. Such a solution would provide the supplier with room to make improvements without the added pressure from an angry customer.

Delivering on such terms can also be a great way for a supplier to show both their integrity and their ability to step up and deliver.

To wrap up this section, my clients' primary goal has always been to complete negotiations, sign the agreement, and then forget about it until renewal. They want it filed away and unseen until then. So, they interpret any reference to the contract before renewal as a sign of trouble.

To avoid this, the best agreements clearly and simply set out the working framework within which both entities will routinely operate. This makes the ongoing relationship more agreeable and allows much stronger customer–client relations to build.

Top Tips

- If your negotiation strategy does not involve playing "hardball" and blocking all concessions, make sure you have a clearly agreed strategy and options for everyone involved.
- Ensure the team recognize those they are about to negotiate with as potential future partners. It will shift the mindset from one that is adversarial and argumentative to something far more positive, ensuring better outcomes.
- The preparation for any negotiation is key to achieving a successful (win-win) outcome. Therefore, ensure that all members of your team are aware in advance of the key areas to fight for and the areas where concessions can be made.

  This should be in terms of both the contractual language and the GI/BAFO positions. Finally, adopt a mindset that is open and flexible.
- Ensure all key stakeholders complete the planning and actions necessary for post-deal delivery of contractual terms. Best practice is to use a formal tracking process to ensure compliance.

CHAPTER 7

Sales and Marketing

Business Modeling

Business modeling (and here I am differentiating it from sales forecasting—see later chapter) is a broad and critically important area, and there are already many offerings in print. Consequently, I am going to offer a limited commentary.

Business modeling is certainly not unusual in either an OEM or after-sales business. It is also fair to say the high number of variables within the latter makes it a challenging proposition.

Of course, there are many types and levels—everything from highly complex models that apply to a whole organization, down to a plan for a specific project or product.

Companies can also undertake business modeling at any time. For example, they could build a plan for a new after-sales service—modeling all aspects of that service from demand, cost, and revenue from Year 1 to the end of its life. Or it could contribute after-sales data to an OEM business model as part of the preparation for a new product line. It can also apply to specific types of complex contracting, such as usage/payment by the hour agreements.

Sometimes, people use this type of modeling to present existing or future financials, while other times it is used to build a business case prior to internal approval.

The quality of business modeling can show wide variance, and, unfortunately, too many either omit critical parameters or contain mathematical errors.

In one extreme case, I witnessed a business that was considering closing one of its most significant sales lines as it was returning only breakeven results.

They spent a considerable amount of time and resources conducting a deep-dive investigation, including a comprehensive analysis of both the commercial and technical aspects.

It was only through the scrutiny of the modeling structure by qualified individuals that the truth emerged, exposing a notable mathematical flaw. Effectively, their proposal pricing and overall business were being undermined by a simple mistake in their core model.

This example illustrates the risks of failing to apply the required time and/or diligence to the process. Time to ensure there are no mistakes in the basic math and diligence to ensure that all the critical-to-task elements have been included.

In a competitive after-sales marketplace, one might expect a typical repairable product-based business model to contain the following as a minimum:

- Product price and cost (Year 1).
- Predicted price and cost escalation (Year 1 onward).
- Investment, margin, and ROI (as appropriate).
- The relevant reliability figures.
- Details of any scheduled maintenance.
- Details of life limitations.
- A time-based projection of market size and profile.
- Projected market capture rate.
- Competitive impacts such as USM, PMA, independent repair schemes, and third-party MRO and spares competitors.

As an example, Figure 7.1 shows the layout for a very basic 10-year business model for a repairable product.

In this example, the shaded cells are user-entry data points for any applicable variables, whereas the plain cells will contain the results of calculations based on those variables.

Every industry will be different, and so businesses need to create their own model template(s) that are both tailored to and truly reflective of the product, service, and marketplace they operate within.

Basic Data	
Date:	
Product Description:	
Part Number:	
Platform Fitted to:	
Qty Per Platform:	
Usage (Hours, Days, etc):	

Variable Data	
Scheduled Maintenance (Y/N):	
Scheduled Maintenance Period (Hours/Days):	
Reliability figure (Removal Rate):	
Average MRO Price:	
Average MRO Cost:	
Competitor Impact:	
Currency Conversion Used:	
Data Confidence Factor:	

Total Product In-service										
	2025	2026	2027	2028	2029	2030	2031	2032	2033	2034
In-service:										
New Deliveries:										
Service Retirement Rate:										
Total Product In-service:										

Product MRO Demand (Qty)										
	2025	2026	2027	2028	2029	2030	2031	2032	2033	2034
MRO:										

Revenue										
	2025	2026	2027	2028	2029	2030	2031	2032	2033	2034
Price Escalation (%):										
Average MRO Price:										
Total MRO Revenue:										

Cost										
	2025	2026	2027	2028	2029	2030	2031	2032	2033	2034
Cost Escalation (%):										
Average MRO Cost:										
Total MRO Cost:										

Summary											
	2025	2026	2027	2028	2029	2030	2031	2032	2033	2034	Total
Total Annual Revenue:											
Total Cumulative Revenue:											
Total Annual Cost:											
Total Cumulative Cost:											
Annual Margin:											
Cumulative Margin:											

Figure 7.1 Example basic business model (repairable product)

Once again, any models applied will need to be regularly reviewed and amended to ensure they keep pace with any changes in the market.

Finally, a truly effective business model reflects all potentially impactful variables as these allow for live testing of "what if," "best case," and "worst case" scenarios, each resulting in different financial outcomes.

Companies can also use such business models as the foundation for value propositions, as discussed in the next chapter.

Top Tips

- Ensure that you have robustly tested any business models that you have created.

  In addition, if they contain extensive formulae and complex math, I recommend seeking independent and suitably qualified experts to assess the efficacy of the model.
- The fact such models exist also necessitates storing them securely and revisiting them routinely.

  It is by having a review process that your business will be able to assess the accuracy of its historic modeling process, track the impact of any changes already made, and learn from any current shortcomings and improve for the future.

Value Propositions

Unless you have a unique and fully protected product/service, the most crucial factor for an after-sales supplier is to have a better overall value proposition than your competitors.

Not only must it be better, but it must also keep pace with the changing dynamic of what customers want and how competitors are innovating to address those requirements.

Driven by the unique nature of each customer and their individual needs and desires, a value proposition will rarely, if ever, have a single thread.

Instead, it will be a combination of elements defined by the product itself, plus the customers and competitors in the market. This could include (but not be limited to) price, speed, communication, quality, reliability, shipping, or any combination of these. For example, an annual cost of ownership cap combined with guaranteed repair and spares lead times.

As previously described, a value proposition must target and be appropriate to whatever is being "sold." For example, when presenting a business (as opposed to a product or service), it would need to address all aspects of that business relevant to the customer's experience and show clear differentiation versus competitors.

For a single product or service, it could be based solely on price differentiation. However, it is not recommended to use this approach as it weakens the competitive position.

It is better to offer multiple areas of differentiation to make it harder for competitors to target.

Ultimately, value propositions are crucial in the sales process and whether they relate directly to your business, or a specific product/service, the importance remains the same.

That said, I have observed that value propositions are often overlooked, and here is an example where I was working with the sales function of an organization:

> Being new to the business, I requested copies of the specific marketing material for each product line.
>
> Over time flyers and brochures were all that I received. Most of them were created many years previously and were of poor quality, with basic errors in presentation and inconsistencies in the messaging.
>
> Worse still, the messaging also failed to provide clear data to demonstrate to the customer why they should be interested in the products.
>
> Eventually, the sales team admitted they had no defined value propositions, and so we started a project to create them.
>
> Unfortunately, it then became clear that they did not even have the basic information. There was no (or very limited) competitor intel (prices, performance, features, etc.) and no recorded data on their customers' needs and challenges.

Now, some market sectors may be less complex and not require such detailed value analysis. However, even in those situations, there must be something that would drive a customer to choose your product or service over others.

> To provide context, the sales process in question was dysfunctional and lacked proper structure, but, surprisingly, the organization considered it successful, as it had been delivering year-on-year growth.

While the historic results were indisputable, without proper control or plan, good fortune had played a significant role in this sales performance. The omissions also meant they were not maximizing their opportunities.

So, just why is this area so important? Well, producing a value proposition forces you to ask the right questions about whatever it is you are trying to sell. It forces you to evaluate yourself against your customers' needs and competitors' offerings. It will provide you with critical intelligence around your customers' expectations and will be a valuable source of the most common reasons for their concerns and, ultimately, rejections.

Sharing a value proposition with a customer can also draw them deeper into the process, lead to meaningful discussions, and engage them in shaping the solution.

By immersing the customer in this way, you are already making significant progress toward achieving a successful sale.

This must be a better way of managing sales as opposed to the disappointingly frequent process of:

Step 1: I make a proposal.
Step 2: You reject it.
Step 3: Return to Step 1.

How do you go about creating a strong value proposition?

- Build a standard template(s) appropriate to your business/market in a spreadsheet at minimum. Best practice is to do this within a CRM; however, the basic structure and content should remain the same regardless of your chosen method and should include the following sections.
- Numbers: Present all the critical financial and any other numerical data from the business model.
  It should include a clear set of assumptions based on your own and any customer, competitor, and market-specific intelligence. This data should be presented in an easily comparable style, whether it is price, cost, reliability, cost of ownership, and so on.

Of course, you would not include costs in any version that you share with a customer. Similarly, if you have been citing any other customer's data, you should respect any commercial confidentiality and either not share it or remove any reference to the source.

- Frequently asked questions (FAQ): Initially, your own team should populate this information and subsequently refine it over time, using any customer feedback and your associated responses.
- USPs: All your product/service USPs, together with a customer comments field for each point.
  Note that as the USP and FAQ data pools expand based on actual life experience and direct customer feedback, they become a valuable resource for improving and perfecting your value propositions.
- Lifecycle: Including the time during which the customer will have/operate the product is critical if there will be ongoing revenue/cost streams.
- Summary: Include an area that brings together and highlights the key elements of the above points.
  This should be a real-time view of the key data elements from the rest of the value proposition to ensure the summary automatically reflects any changes in the back-office data.

Think for a moment about how useful these data would be if it were available to your sales team in real-time. Just imagine the power of being able to update their sales positions while they are out visiting your customers.

Proactively enhancing value propositions reduces the need for proposal changes and subsequent return travel to the client. This will save your business valuable cost and time.

All too often, I have seen sales teams working with poorly defined value propositions, and yes, as discussed here, sometimes, with none! With the latter situation, the sales team typically "flies by the seat of their pants," relying on experience but with no real understanding or direction. Unfortunately, this usually results in the sales activity becoming increasingly transactional and significantly more challenging.

Top Tips

- No business should allow salespeople to work with their customers without defined and appropriately tailored value propositions.

  Instead, drive the best and most productive behaviors within your sales team by ensuring they always have the right tools to present your products and services in the most positive light.

Unique Selling Points

"If you don't distinguish yourself from the crowd, you'll just be the crowd,"

—Rebecca Mark, former head of Enron International,
and President of Resource Development Partners.

A successful USP will present a clear and meaningful benefit to your customers and make your product, service, and/or brand stand out from the competition in some unique way. It is essentially the value you offer and/or the problem you solve for your customers that your competitors do not.

Failing to present that differentiation means the options for the customer are all the same—your offering has no merit over whatever anyone else is offering. Without differentiation, you are leaving the decision-making to your customers based on their own understanding, prejudices, and bias.

Therefore, investing time and effort into this critical area can reap dividends. Unfortunately, many organizations put far too little effort into differentiating their business from their competitors.

One business was struggling to get traction with new customers and so failing to meet the required progress against their sales targets.

We set up a workshop, and, after collecting customer feedback and conducting a line-by-line comparison against both reality and their competitors, we discovered issues with what they believed were three of their key USPs:

- TAT and spares delivery performance had fallen behind what their competitors were routinely offering.
- Their product reliability was significantly below that of their competitors.
- They were promising customers high levels of customer service and routine purchase order–status reporting, but their customer service team was overwhelmed and unable to provide this consistently.

In summary, the organization's failure to meet three of their critical USPs (which were also the most important requirements for their customers) resulted in a decline in sales.

They had mistakenly convinced themselves that they knew what their customers wanted and that they were delivering it.

The inability of many organizations to identify true USPs suggests this task should not be taken lightly. Often, organizations fail to undertake external verification of their perceived value or relevance to customers when defining basic product features and/or service quality–related claims as USPs.

Therefore, when developing USPs, an organization should pay close attention to the following simple steps:

1. Identify what the customer wants and needs now and what their current (and potential future) challenges are.
2. Identify what customers most value about your competitors' existing products and services.
3. Rank the above responses in order of importance to your customers. Once you have the final list, identify those product and service elements that are both meaningful to your customers and not offered by your customers.

4. Complete a SWOT (Strengths, Weaknesses, Opportunities, and Threats) analysis that shows those areas where your competitors have clear differentiation from your business.

   Identify how many and how critical your competitors' unique strengths are to your customers. This will also define the improvement actions you need to take and, potentially, whether you should even remain in the market.

   If there are competitor weaknesses, then, by targeting these, you are already closing in on potential USPs.

Finally, and perhaps the most difficult tasks are:

5. Identify the direction of the market.
6. Brainstorm to uncover as-yet-unidentified problems or benefits.

Many ways exist for forming USPs, and, sometimes, the answers can be very simple, for example:

- If your price is higher than your competitors, but your reliability and product life are better, use the latter to determine the true cost of ownership. This can serve as a significant USP.
- When you take your competitors as a group, it is possible that your USPs might appear to be the same as theirs. However, when you consider each of your competitors individually, how many still have the same USPs as you?

   If they do, how do you create the required differentiation?

   One way might be to wrap commercial terms around your USPs, for example, if you have slick shipping or fast MRO TAT, or great product reliability, why not guarantee it?

   This way, while you still have the same basic USPs as your competitor, you are varying the presentation and creating something unique.

Even in noncompetitive markets, we should be "baiting the hook for our customers" as it should be our aim to use USPs to both encourage and influence customer buying decisions.

But, whatever the result, an organization must present these differences in a way that illustrates its offering in a better light than its competitors.

Top Tips

- Creating USPs can be a challenge, so involve creative and lateral thinkers and always, always ensure that any ideas really will add value when viewed from a customer's perspective.
- Ensure that customers can easily understand any USPs—written clearly and concisely and so they can directly relate to them.
- As I have already stated many times, do not lose sight of the simple fact that all customers are different. Therefore, while USPs can (and do) work across an entire market, also be prepared to consider tailoring the approach to specific customers.

Sales

You have your product and/or service ready. You have old lapsed, new, and target customers identified, and you have a sales team—so you are ready to go, right? The answer is "*in theory, yes*"; however, the sales activity is a lot more complex than that.

Let us start with the salesperson—typically, they are free spirits and enjoy being out on the road, travelling, meeting, and socializing with your customers. However, I have rarely met any who enjoy doing the hard yards back at base, be that sales preparation, proposal generation, visit planning and reports, sales forecasting, post-sales follow-up, and so on.

In fact, many salespeople see any time spent back at base as a waste of their valuable time, and, unfortunately, many organizations subscribe to that view.

Effectively, this is the often-said "If they're not out selling, they are of no value to me" approach. This is not a rare phenomenon either, as I have seen many organizations that lacked the sales processes, KPIs, and ability to manage the sales team and vital intelligence effectively. Essentially, they left the sales team alone to self-manage their activities because "they get results."

This approach can work to an extent, but it will also usually exhibit unhelpful traits such as being very reactive, having little detailed planning, low levels of accountability, and suboptimal results.

Eventually, there will be a point of failure. This could occur when someone recognizes the lack of ROI delivered by the sales effort, or when one of the sales team leaves suddenly. With the latter, losing headcount is not the only concern. Whereas finding a replacement may be relatively easy, losing critical customer, market, and project knowledge could create a significant gap in your sales activities.

So, I can guarantee that a sales process without efficient structure and systems in place will never provide optimal returns on a sustainable basis.

To assist with your thinking on this subject, I am going to pose some simple questions related to the fundamentals of sales:

- Is your business hitting its sales targets and are your customers happy?
- Have you provided your sales team with training on both the products and services they are selling, plus effective sales and negotiation techniques?
- If you are selling highly engineered, or technically complex products, have you ensured that your sales team has the right background (technically literate)?
- Does your business have suitable up-to-date promotional material and website/portal and social media to support the sales team? Is everything updated regularly?
- Have you considered how to reach potential customers you cannot directly access and ensure they understand your messaging through non-F2F methods, such as hard-copy and social media?
- Do you have an ongoing process for identifying your target customers, and how do you prioritize them for the sales team's attention?
- Does each of your sales team have an agreed customer visit plan that optimizes the travel to achieve maximum customer interactions in the most efficient manner, delivering the best results from the incurred expense?

- Is there a clear policy on budget allocation for T&E (travel and entertaining), clear user guidelines, and a simple authorization process?
- To ensure that the sales team has completed all their required preparation before they leave the office, is there a previsit checklist in place?
- Is there a standard post–sales visit reporting process, and, if so, is the information (and any actions) stored and shared internally?
- Do you store all your customer contact data (names, telephone, e-mail, addresses, etc.) centrally (and therefore available to all)?
- Are you tracking the activities and timescales associated with post–sales visit/meeting action items?
- Do your salespeople have clear KPIs relating to visit planning, sales, contract targets, win rates, T&E, and so on? Are there regular updates to allow each of these targets to be monitored against progress gates and actual results?
- Have you provided your sales team with the appropriate e-tools, for example, online access to marketing media, sales order status, C-Sat info, RFP/RFQ status, and so on to allow them to undertake their role effectively?

If your answer to any question is "no," I would suggest you have work to do, and, if you answered "no" to the second bullet, then shame on you!

While some might argue that great salespeople are born with their abilities, being successful in sales requires a diverse range of skills. Certain traits like confidence, communication, and listening skills may come naturally to some individuals. In contrast, other crucial elements, such as time management, preparation, negotiation, and closing skills, need to be learned and developed through training.

That is why both sales process and specific business product/service training are fundamental to having successful salespeople in your business.

It is also crucial to recognize that sales personnel represent a significant operational expense; therefore, optimizing their efficacy necessitates investment in appropriate resources and support systems.

Having looked at the organizational process, there is also value in examining the behaviors within the actual sales activity itself. Again, these are not theoretical statements but actual examples of poor sales process and technique that I have regularly witnessed:

Failing to Apply the five "Ps" (Perfect Preparation Prevents Poor Performance)

For me, this applies to absolutely every element of sales activity, be that turning up on time, in presentable/appropriate attire and with all the required information, and so on.

Failing to Build a Compelling Value Proposition

There are two key factors that need to be addressed in constructing value propositions.

The first is that many salespeople fail to do their due diligence before presenting a list of USPs and features/benefits, resulting in pitches that are not relevant to the customer.

Second, it is vital to recognize the significance of "service"—salespeople cannot effectively meet their goals if their carefully crafted position is being undermined by their business having unsatisfactory service levels and dissatisfied customers.

Poor-Quality Presentation/Proposal Material

Providing anything that contains errors, be that presentation or proposal material, is unacceptable.

Let me be very clear—first impressions really count. A salesperson serves as a window into a business, and, if they cannot be bothered to prepare professionally, it speaks volumes for the business.

Failing to Practice/Test

It is disheartening to see salespeople visit customers without even conducting a dry run of their material internally, demonstrating both overconfidence and laziness.

The very best organizations routinely engage in role-play to ensure they polish and professionalize their sales activities.

Not Understanding the Subject Matter

I can confirm from painful experience that there is nothing worse than witnessing a salesperson attempt to bluff their way through a presentation because of lack of preparation.

Sometimes, they may be trying to sell a new product line or products so complex they are outside of their technical capacity. In such circumstances, it would be understandable why an individual might not have a full grasp of the subject. However, if they had completed their pre-trip preparation, they would have understood the challenge. They could have either proactively explained the limitation to the customer, or developed a remedial plan, such as being accompanied by a subject-matter expert.

Failing to Have a Plan B (and Plan C)

Have you ever arrived at a customer's facility for a sales pitch, only to find their conference-room screen is not working and you did not bring hardcopies for your audience? Or the purchasing team you were supposed to be meeting now includes the CFO, who has a list of questions and issues you are unprepared for.

So, never, ever forget the quote from motivational speaker, writer, and consultant, Denis Waitley—"Expect the best, plan for the worst, and prepare to be surprised."

Inadequate or Missing KPIs

If a company incentivizes sales or commercial employees with bonuses based on their performance, deploying no or poorly focused KPIs can cause suboptimal outcomes. For example, they may not reward your sales personnel to secure deals at the GI level (ensuring optimum returns for your business).

In such cases, the negotiating team can opt for the BAFO "path of least resistance" to secure the win (and their bonus) without fear of repercussions, and your business ends up with poorer results.

Not Listening

Too many times, employers hire salespeople based on the mistaken assumption that good talkers are also good listeners, but this is not always the case. Instead, while communication should be a two-way activity, in the worst examples, the ability to talk (transmitting) means there is no time left for listening (receiving).

Customers feel immense frustration when they explain their issues and the salesperson fails to acknowledge and reflect their concerns, sticking strictly to their script. Whereas, the best salespeople probe, listen, and digest first. Then they will adapt as necessary to negotiate any obstacles proactively. If they cannot do that on the spot, they exit and return to base for further discussion, review, and, if possible, realignment of the offering. What they never do is just keep presenting the same offering covered in slightly different-colored wrapping.

Pitching to the Wrong Person

Falling directly into the area of the five "Ps" is wasting time and effort pitching to the wrong audience. This is a fundamental failure to understand a customer's hierarchy and decision-making process.

Making Assumptions

Apart from the preceding point, maybe there are multiple stakeholders and decision-makers in the customer process.

Avoid focusing your material on purely those who might be present in the face-to-face meetings. For example, you may meet with an engineering team and so will have built a technical presentation/proposal. But what happens after you have left, and they submit your bid internally for senior management to review?

You may assume that their engineering team will "make the sale" internally for you. But in doing so, you are letting a third party act on your behalf, with all the inherent risks of loss of emphasis and understanding that can negatively impact your messaging.

Of course, it is still perfectly viable to tailor the verbal/visual presentation to your immediate audience. But just ensure that you structure any material you plan to leave behind in a way that enables the customer's stakeholders across functions and at multiple levels to comprehend the key messages.

For key bids, conducting a dry run with personnel from different areas of your business can be a great way to test the clarity of your messaging.

Failing to Follow Up and Close

Unfortunately, poor personal time management and lack of process controls can mean sales bids being overlooked with a subsequent negative impact on win rate. Bonuses and poor KPIs can also contribute to a dysfunctional deal-closing process.

Great salespeople are typically perseverant, but they sometimes become overly focused on chasing personal recognition (be that a simple desire for acknowledgment and/or financial reward).

This manifests itself in a tendency to move on too quickly and a reluctance to do the "hard yards" to drive a challenging sale over the line. Once again, the negotiating team can follow the path of least resistance, and that will never deliver the best returns.

Even the most successful salespeople who achieve great win rates and where others mutter about the fact they must be mind readers—they are not. Instead, they are very adept at asking the right questions in subtle ways that tease out specific information they need. They then thoroughly analyze these conversations until they have extracted every useful piece of information.

To summarize, what makes a great salesperson? Well, the very best—and this really applies to any customer-facing personnel—possess a natural ability to "read the room" and react accordingly.

These social/emotional chameleons can quickly develop situational awareness in any setting and then change their approach to create empathy with customers (and colleagues). Outstanding salespeople also have an ego drive that makes them both want and need to make the sale—they have a need to conquer and win (Mayer and Greenberg 2006, 2).

Combining these skills with active listening, trust building, strong relationship creation, and effective negotiation creates a winning skill set.

The great salesperson will have also received full-service, product, and vocational training. They will prepare diligently, including dry runs and putting themselves in their customer's shoes when critiquing the proposal and/or any presentation material.

This preparation will have ensured a comprehensive understanding of their audience and the product and service they are offering.

They will thoroughly understand the value proposition and commercial options, enabling them to discuss and negotiate to closure confidently.

They will pursue the opportunity relentlessly until they either close it as a win or a loss.

Finally, they will make sure to document and internally share the key reasons the deal was won (or lost).

Top Tips

- Do not be afraid to have those tough conversations with your customers. Instead, meet the challenge head-on, engage in open and probing discussions that remove guesswork and assumption from the process, and utilize the information like the liquid gold that it is.
- There are no shortcuts to winning. Instead, all successful sales efforts must be based on diligent planning, effort, and employees who are prepared to "do the hard yards."

Sales Forecasting

The first thing you must recognize is that any type of business forecast is inherently inaccurate.

Why is this the case? Well, they are based only on the information you have available to you at that specific moment in time. You may assume that you have every piece of information that can impact the forecast in the future. However, this is flawed thinking, as you can never control the future actions of all the external stakeholders, or the operating environment within which you work.

The following statement aptly summarizes the subject: "The goal of forecasting is not to predict the future but to tell you what you need to know to take meaningful action in the present" (Saffo 2007, 1).

Markets, competitors, economics, customers, suppliers, technology, regulation, and so on can all intervene (and frequently do) to render today's forecast inaccurate. It is, therefore, just a question of by how much and in which direction this will manifest itself.

That said, you also cannot operate any business effectively without a sales forecast, as without this vital assessment, how can you plan the level of inventory, resources, and infrastructure, and so on?

So, while they represent a challenge, we must also recognize the advantages of having a fully functioning and ongoing forecasting process in place. Yes, the initial setup can be time-consuming, but once the framework is in place, the ongoing upkeep becomes much more efficient.

Many business sectors have a natural ebb and flow to them and there are also many external factors that can cause sales to rise and fall.

On each occasion a fall occurs, business leadership will urgently want to know what is happening and what remedial action will be taken to address the situation. Businesses consider fast access to such information crucial, but, without a strong forecasting process, they will need to engage in extensive, manual, and case-by-case data-mining to uncover those insights.

Of course, this is all reactive, rearview-mirror activity, and while that necessary investigative work continues, it is highly probable you will also have your sales team engaged in the activity.

So, while sales are falling, the one team that can help turn that around will be back at base analyzing data and "belly button gazing."

Here is an example of what can happen when it goes wrong:

The sales of a specific business, which had an annual budget in the multimillion-dollar range, were showing a significant downturn.

The decrease was completely opposite to the increasing trend projected in their forecast, leaving them perplexed.

Here, the initial investigative requirements were:

1. Generate a breakdown of recent and current year sales by customer and product.
2. Produce a copy of the current detailed sales forecast.

3. Overlay the actual sales and forecast sales data, identifying any shortfalls or trends.

The request was made for these reports, and the actual sales data were provided in due course, but the sales forecast was missing. Subsequently, the organization admitted that this did not exist, and so, the next obvious question was—"If you don't have a detailed sales forecast, then how did you build this year's budget?"

You might already be ahead of me with the answer. "We took last year's total actual sales and added the forecasted price escalation for the year, along with a percentage growth figure from the board."

So, the problem became obvious—a multimillion-dollar business with no detailed plan of where their sales were going to come from.

I have kept my discussions as "vanilla" as possible regarding the market involved, as the points being made are non–industry segment specific. However, I am now about to break that rule to put this next point in context and make it clearer for you to understand.

In the aerospace market, when an aircraft is in its production phase, forecasting the fleet size in service and, therefore, likely after-sales demand, is, by comparison, a relatively straightforward process. However, once an aircraft type is no longer being manufactured, it becomes OOP and everything changes.

As the aircraft age, they begin retiring from service. With modern practices, companies recycle a significant portion of the products installed on each retired aircraft. These recycled products then enter the market as USM.

Recycling means the OEM, having already stopped new production, now faces reducing after-sales spares demand as well.

Dealing with low and highly variable demand is usually not a strength of OEMs. Consequently, they struggle to control manufacturing costs, which can lead to rapid price increases.

This means the products become far more attractive targets to competitors who can manufacture cheaper copy parts under the PMA process.

All these activities will have a detrimental effect on an OEM's *after-market* sales by depressing demand for new spares and MRO.

To provide more context, it is important to note that platform data, specifically aircraft type, are crucial in the aerospace market. This is because manufacturers typically design each product for a specific aircraft platform. For example, a valve, part number 123456-23, is only fitted to the Boeing 757 platform.

I will now return to the example started above:

The next challenge, unfortunately, was the incompleteness of the historical sales data; vital information was absent. For example, while they had all the product part number and description information, the platform data were sparse.

In fact, approximately 50 percent of the spares sold had no platform data allocated. This was repeated against the MRO data, albeit on a smaller scale.

Finally, there were also significant errors with the platforms. First, there were many misallocations of the spares and MRO orders; for example, Boeing 757–specific product was identified as Boeing 747. Second, products were mistakenly categorized across the market segments.

In due course, investigations revealed that the overall lack of accuracy within the product *master data* structure was undermining the ability to analyze the market/customer trends.

In fact, as the daily ongoing order administration continued to refer to that same data source, it was recognized that without remedial action the problem was only going to get worse.

The project involved a master data review and update. This helped ensure accuracy for new sales order data, although historic data issues remained unresolved.

For the historic sales data, which ran to tens of thousands of order lines, these all needed to be corrected before any detailed analysis could even begin. To add to the pain, all the analysis had to be completed offline in spreadsheets from two old ERP systems. It took more than a month of scrubbing before the data was clean and the analysis was completed.

The findings eventually revealed the background to the sharp sales decline:

- This organization had hundreds of primary products comprising many thousands of individual piece parts. But it surprised them to find that one product generated roughly 40 percent of their MRO and spare parts sales.

  They had also failed to recognize it was a legacy product fitted to an older generation of OOP aircraft, where the in-service fleet was already in decline and USM was an increasing competitive reality.

- The business had also failed to understand the danger inherent in the compound effect of uncontrolled escalations on their spares pricing that had been applied over many years.

  As a result, the product had reached a significant price-to-cost differential.

- The OEM's inability to manufacture the product on a reliable schedule consistently caused late delivery of spares orders to customers by the after-sales team.

- Customer support had also failed to address (or escalate to senior management) the increasingly stressed complaints from their customers about both the price and delivery performance.

  Those complainants included their primary customer of the product, who just happened to have extensive in-house engineering capability and a reputation for making their own parts.

So, a lack of market knowledge, a high product price, ongoing poor spares delivery, and poor customer support combined to create a "perfect storm."

The outcome was a sharp decrease in sales for their most important product. This was because their primary customer designed and manufactured an authorized copy (PMA), as well as a general market shift toward USM instead of new spares and MRO.

To further add to the problems:

- Their sales were heavily legacy product reliant, and, unfortunately, several were also reaching the end of their service life.

Without the detail, they had no basis upon which to monitor ongoing actual versus forecast sales at the customer and product level. Therefore, the business was slow to recognize that sales had not only become flat but had begun to decline across other important product lines.

Finally, they had also been expecting the deliveries of their next generation of new products to underpin sales growth continuity. However, they had failed to factor in the effect of the extended warranty periods that existed on these new products and that these would suppress sales for an extended period.

Of course, hindsight is a wonderful thing, and I recognize that even if they had a detailed bottom-up forecast, it would not have fully negated the impact on sales. But if they had such a process, they would have been significantly better-informed and aware of each of their products' position in the marketplace.

They could have already modeled various market assumptions, significantly better understood them, and reflected them in the organization's sales forecast. They would have been able to recognize their sales risk from being heavily single and legacy product reliant and understood the impact of warranty on revenue streams.

With the benefit of such key data, they would have been able to instigate preventative/remedial actions far earlier.

So, just how do you create a simple sales forecasting process?

Well, the first point to make is that customers purchase products and services and not dollars.

A sales team should, wherever possible, be forecasting at the lowest level of demand, that is, quantity of products. Product demand (forecast) data should be overlaid with standard pricing data; that is, each item should have a price allocated to it to create the sales forecast.

In situations where there is a distinction in prices for different customers, particularly in cases involving variable spares and MRO pricing, companies should use the actual pricing applicable to each customer. However, this can also involve a considerable amount of complexity.

A simpler, less accurate, but directionally indicative model using a single price (usually an average) per product can also be used as an alternative.

Multiplying the two datasets together will produce a simple demand and sales value file. Depending on the datasets used, this file can be the basis for various types of analysis, such as sales by customer, product, platform, and so on. Including a calendar within the file will allow the sales to be broken down by month/week and so on. Once the base data file is complete, ensure that it reflects the market by including any specific variables as clearly stated assumptions. For example, in the aerospace market, this would include items like platform retirement rate, product retirement-to-USM conversion rate, PMA activity, price escalation, and so on.

Following the development and budgetary approval of a robust forecasting model, it serves as the principal benchmark for monitoring actual sales performance.

Ideally, there will also be an ongoing review process to confirm that the assumptions used in the forecast model represent what is happening in the marketplace.

Creating such a forecast is a significant task and certainly not something to be undertaken as an ad hoc exercise. The ideal position is to build a repeatable process with clean master data, automatic base data acquisition, and adjustable assumptions to reflect market variables.

While monthly financial reporting is standard business practice, the manual sales review and forecasting processes are labor intensive. Transferring data from ERP systems to offline tools such as spreadsheets creates considerable challenges.

Therefore, I would always recommend setting up this process within your existing business ERP system, or ideally, via a CRM that has built-in links to your ERP. This will have the advantage of automating a significant element of the activity. In fact, many of today's CRM suppliers include AI-based sales tools within their software packages, making forecasting a significantly more efficient process.

Per my earlier comments, best practice involves conducting an initial primary data cleanup, as regardless of the system chosen, this one-time effort will establish data integrity for all subsequent years. The good news is that there are now software tools and AI available to assist with what has been a painful task historically.

One last point is that whether you use ERP or CRM as the tool, it must be able to track and timestamp any changes to the forecast. This will provide far greater control and subsequent insight as the forecast develops.

Once you create a detailed "by product/by customer" forecast, it becomes very easy to build KPIs around it. These can then drive the behaviors of your sales people, as they will be monitored at the appropriate level.

From direct experience, I know that deploying such a structure ensures there will be more proactive monitoring and questioning of customers whenever variance to budget is evident.

So, this system has three major benefits for your sales team. First, it equips them with critical sales data. Second, it helps drive their focus. And third, it provides them with the data to enable "smart" questioning of their customers.

The result is a system that will not only improve the overall actions of your sales team but also significantly improve the market intelligence available to your business.

A business also benefits from correctly setting up forecasting because any S&OP system will require a demand forecast as part of its foundations.

Having run "bottom-up" forecasts in many businesses, I can certainly attest to the benefits they deliver to the sales team's operation and effectiveness.

Back in the day, both annual, five and ten-year-plan forecasting was a manual, spreadsheet-driven process that caused endless pain and headaches for the salespeople. It diverted their focus away from external matters and made them overly introspective.

However, with modern business management and CRM, there has been a major step forward. These systems empower businesses to build automated tools that streamline data preparation and analysis. AI is now also augmenting sales forecasting, and these advances are combining to significantly improve both the process and the sales team's support.

The action of linking forecasting to KPIs and using it going forward has another very significant advantage. By routinely reviewing and adjusting your forecast, you can maintain a rolling window that spans 12 to 24 months or longer, depending on your needs.

Maintaining this "live" and current forecast means it is regularly and incrementally adjusted to reflect the realities of market dynamics. This incremental approach eliminates both the usual resource stress and large data swings associated with typical half year and annual forecasting updates.

Finally, because the sales team will use factual market intelligence to produce the detailed "bottom-up" forecast, they will remove emotion and conjecture from the assessment. This will improve the accuracy of the information and subsequent decisions within a business.

The final part of this chapter relates to the models. Many businesses still forecast their sales activity at the financial and customer level. However, they often face structural weaknesses in converting the sales forecast into a meaningful demand for parts or services. As I have already stated, it is far better to have the sales team forecast at a quantity level (units as opposed to financial values).

Using the same example as the baseline, the following will provide you with a quick historical recap of how the presentation of simple sales forecasts has progressed.

The journey begins with the type of historical spares sales forecast that I first saw early in my career and ends with today's "best practice" overarching demand-based sales forecast.

Of course, current forecasting practices have rightly increased in complexity. However, it is fair to say the level of data (and accuracy) now available will be significantly more beneficial to a business than ever before.

In Figure 7.2, we have an early example of a spares sales forecast, showcasing the projected 45 percent growth of a fictional customer named "Example Business A," across a four-year period. However, the forecast also contains very limited useful information for the supplier.

In Figure 7.3, the sales data break down to another level, providing a clear depiction of the sales value for each line of product that Business A

	Sales Revenue (£GBP)			
	Actuals			Forecast
Customer	2022	2023	2024	2025
Example Business A	£63,316	£53,732	£54,377	£91,676

Figure 7.2 Simple customer-level sales revenue forecast

Customer	Product Pt. No.	Sales Revenue (£GBP)			
		Actuals			Forecast
		2022	2023	2024	2025
Example Business A	578231	£0	£0	£0	£20,000
Example Business A	539007	£23,976	£31,552	£42,075	£66,899
Example Business A	227614	£2,300	£2,750	£3,294	£4,776
Example Business A	178666	£7,040	£3,770	£1,736	£0
Example Business A	734219	£30,000	£15,660	£7,272	£0
		£63,316	£53,732	£54,377	£91,676

Figure 7.3 Simple customer- and product-based spares revenue forecast

Customer	Product Pt. No.	Demand (Qty)			
		Actuals			Forecast
		2022	2023	2024	2025
Example Business A	578231	0	0	0	100
Example Business A	539007	74	136	153	230
Example Business A	227614	50	55	61	88
Example Business A	178666	110	65	31	0
Example Business A	734219	30	18	12	0
		264	274	257	418

Figure 7.4 Simple demand (quantity)–based sales forecast

is purchasing. Every customer of the business would undergo this type of analysis, which is certainly more useful as it reveals the sales trajectory by product (albeit at a cash level).

Figure 7.4 presents a different approach as the sales team focuses on a demand forecast, which will certainly be more meaningful for the organization's operational departments (manufacturing, spares, shopfloor, etc.).

In Figure 7.5, we have a current example of a simple "best practice" forecast. It contains all the basic information a business needs to operate—including demand, sales, intel, and so on.

This is a basic tool because users can also include other pieces of information, including confidence factoring and annual price escalation, and so on.

With forecasting, there are many different formats, tools, and vehicles. These include everything from ERP system, to CRM, to spreadsheet, and everything between. The most comprehensive and effective approach I have found combines S&OP with CRM integration.

Customer	Product Pt. No.	Average Price (£GBP)			2025 List Price	Demand (Qty)				Sales Revenue (£GBP)				Sales Commentary / Intel
		2022	2023	2024	2025	Actuals			Forecast	Actuals			Forecast	
						2022	2023	2024	2025	2022	2023	2024	2025	
Example Business A	578231	£0	£0	£0	£200	0	0	0	100	£0		£0	£20,000	Major new distribution agreement launched end December 2024. Forecasting sales of around £20k in 2025
Example Business A	539007	£324	£232	£275	£292	74	136	153	230	£23,976	£31,552	£42,075	£66,899	The customers blue riband product—they expect to deliver 50% growth in demand in 2025 and 40% in 2026
Example Business A	227614	£46	£50	£54	£54	50	55	61	88	£2,300	£2,750	£3,294	£4,776	Historically demand has been growing around 10% p.a. but the customer is forecasting 45% for 2025
Example Business A	178666	£64	£58	£56	£58	110	65	31	0	£7,040	£3,770	£1,736	£0	Lost the distribution rights to their main competitor
Example Business A	734219	£1,000	£870	£606	£0	30	18	12	0	£30,000	£15,660	£7,272	£0	Product has been superceded and will end production in Q3 2024
						264	274	257	418	£63,316	£53,732	£54,377	£91,676	

Figure 7.5 Simple modern spares demand and revenue forecast

Top Tips

- As we have discussed, a forecast represents your best estimate of what is expected to happen. Overlaying it with live data will not only provide a resource to track daily performance but also highlight areas requiring further investigation or action.
- Never view a forecast as a one-time historic document (unless it is superseded). Instead, it should be a live entity that continuously updates with the very latest, best intelligence available and, thus, reflects the current realities of the marketplace.
- Sandbagging (the act of the sales team under forecasting to establish a low sales target in order to achieve greater-than-expected results) still occurs far too often.

  Typically, the sales team deploys this strategy when they receive incentives for their results and when there is a weak forecasting process in place. It can be a major impediment to forecast accuracy, and so it is imperative that all personnel taking part in the process be incentivized to maintain transparency and honesty. This should apply regardless of whether the news is good or bad.

  Openly acknowledging and addressing sandbagging, when identified, ensures everyone understands its unacceptability.

Competition

Any book on after-sales would be remiss not to address the negative effects competition can have on your business.

It may seem obvious, but it is worth stating—doing the basics well and consistently should be the first line of defense for your business. This refers to the service elements (delivery communication, support, etc.) associated with customer satisfaction. Failure to ensure that the fundamentals are in place leaves a business vulnerable to attack and, at best, leads to the Leaky Bucket Syndrome referred to earlier.

The commercial aerospace market is a good example of how failing to follow this advice can cause the proliferation of competition and associated loss of market share to competitors. When commercial aero-space began, the supply chain was short; just the OEM with a direct link to the customer (airlines). Sometimes, this occurred via an OEM after-sales division, as shown by the two solid block arrows in Figure 7.6. Years of challenges, including those discussed in this book, have led to a substantial loss of market share for OEMs and their aftermarket divisions to their competitors. This is clearly visible in the chaotic supply chain spaghetti that exists today. This is a prime example of the damage caused when the response to competition is not being managed effectively and service levels are below the levels needed to deliver customer satisfaction.

To be clear, I am not suggesting complete prevention would have been possible, since the original OEM dominance was bound to erode. However, I can confidently say that there could have been a significantly reduced breadth, depth, and speed of the impact. That said, competition and the challenge it generates in after-sales will remain a constant threat, regardless of whether you are OEM-owned or an independent supplier. Additionally, while great service should be a primary defense, it will never provide complete immunity from competitive market pressure. It is quite literally a perpetual fight for survival.

Despite its importance, competition is also an oddity because of the reactions it generates. My observations are that organizations fall into one of three camps. The first camp views it as a bad thing and responds with negativity, wasting time and effort that could otherwise be spent taking positive action to deal with the challenge. Focusing heavily on their own business, the second camp is simply complacent to it. The third camp embraces it and reflects the words of Arie de Geus, the former head of Royal Dutch Shell's Strategic Planning Group: "The ability to learn faster than your competitors may be the only sustainable competitive advantage." So, the third group looks upon competition as a positive driving force in their business. They understand that it both stops them from becoming complacent and delivers critical value.

One specific value that is often deployed successfully is to work collaboratively with competitors. This obviously requires the establishment and maintenance of cordial relations, but there is real value to be taken from it. For instance, in the aerospace market, the sharing of market and customer intelligence and mutual inventory support are commonplace.

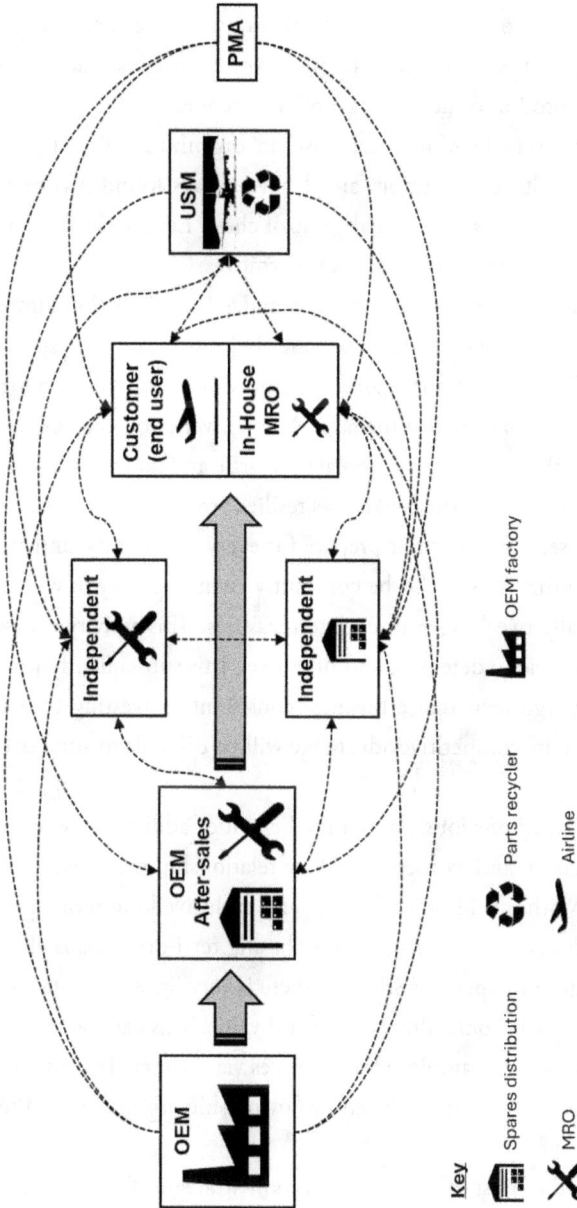

Figure 7.6 Today's decentralized commercial aerospace supply chain

Key

Spares distribution

MRO

Parts recycler

Airline

OEM factory

Furthermore, despite inherent risks, the prevalence of "co-opetition"—cooperative competition—is growing across multiple industries (Brandenburger and Nalebuff 2021, 4).

My observations with multiple organizations are that being in the third group and leveraging competition to fuel progress and growth has undeniably produced the most favorable outcomes.

It can be very helpful to establish an organizational culture that is comfortable with competition, and I have always found it beneficial to present the subject as a perpetual game of chess. Effectively, it is an ongoing game of strategy, moves, and countermoves.

So, just how can you prepare for and counter all the competitive threats to your business? Well, you can obviously react on a spot, or "as they occur" basis, but that can make for a very reactive organization, which can be exhausting to manage. Alternatively, you can acknowledge the fact that these competitive threats will arise and take proactive steps to prepare your business and make it as resilient to attack as you can.

Of course, you can never prepare for every eventuality, and, as these competitive threats will also be constantly changing, so you will need to be continually tweaking your countermeasures. This activity can be broken into two parts: defensive and offensive. This subsequently presents a compelling argument that a business consistently investing to maintain and enhance its competitive advantage will be difficult to surpass (Porter 2004, 482).

I have talked previously about the benefit of adding value to the purchasing decision and, consequently, the relationship that exists with your customer. Without this and if there is no exclusive long-term agreement in place, you are in transactional purchasing territory. This is always the riskiest ground to operate within, as there is very little to create customer loyalty. The goal should always be to add value. This can be through tangible methods, for example, added services via the servitization model, or it can be abstract, for example, cost of ownership arguments and so on.

One of the most effective servitization strategies I have seen was marketed to the customer as "making their life easier" and "giving them cash." What it actually did was to increase the customer's dependence on the supplier.

The supplier achieved this by deploying several additional services. This included purchasing a section of the customers' inventory, which was then left in situ at the customer site. This had multiple benefits for the customer, including shortening their supply chain, a cash injection for the inventory they sold, and lower ongoing costs from their reduced inventory holding. The supplier received payment for each inventory item at the point of customer transaction.

The customer in question was also very sensitive to product reliability, and so the supplier provided additional onsite technical support. These services moved the supplier up the supply chain and achieved the intended aim of increasing the customer's reliance on them. Over time, this created a much stronger supplier–client relationship and presented competitors with a significantly higher entry barrier.

In the following examples, I will present (in no order) some methods that I have seen successfully deployed to defend against competition:

Price Cuts
While offering price discounts can be a successful strategy, there are also potential risks, for example:

- Price reductions in response to direct competition may see customers choosing the competitor regardless of any action you might take. Effectively, the customer recognizes and rewards the positive outcome caused by the "disruptor."
- If the discount is too deep, your customers may react negatively, concluding that the original price must have been too high.

It is good practice to frame price discounts as the result of another action. For instance, "we have managed to reduce our material costs and so we can now cut our prices." This helps to negate the customers' "the price must have been too high" argument.

Cost of Ownership

It can be too easy to prioritize price reductions when faced with competition or declining sales. Therefore, it is important to consider presenting an alternative view based on the total cost of ownership to your customers if there are ongoing costs associated with your products/services, such as MRO. This can be great for differentiating the potential for long-term cost savings versus a competitor's lower initial sticker price. This argument will not persuade all customers (even if it is extremely compelling) as some simply prioritize lower upfront costs, even if it means paying more in the long-term. Nevertheless, this can be a very enticing approach for many customers.

Fair Pricing

You can choose to implement a pricing strategy that ensures the difference between the price and the cost does not reach the point where it can be viewed as "unfair." Effectively, you will manage pricing to avoid the "fairness" trigger point being reached by keeping the margin lower. At the same time, you will make the competitive space less attractive to new entrants.

Exclusivity

Achieving an exclusive supply agreement with a customer is, of course, one of the most effective ways of fending off competitors. However, while it can be a useful target to secure key and strategic accounts, it is very unlikely to act as a complete firewall for any business. This is predominantly because establishing dominance in a market potentially strays into the legal implications of anti-competitive conduct.

It is also worth noting that customers can be risk-averse with their business operations and can view aligning themselves with a single supplier (sole source) as being a step too far. From a supplier's perspective, securing exclusivity is likely to require greater commercial incentives for the customer and being prepared to include a temporary break clause for any period of noncontractual delivery. Essentially, this gives the customer some comfort that if there are delivery challenges, they can seek solutions from alternative suppliers during the period of nonperformance.

Redesign

A simple redesign of a product or service—incorporating new features and benefits, can create a new value proposition and deliver competitive advantage. However, any changes introduced must deliver actual benefit to the customer and not just be "decorative" additions.

It is important to mention that any price increase or introduction fees resulting from the alterations may lead to some customers declining the changes, regardless of the potential advantages. Consequently, this strategy may not be a complete solution.

Financial Incentives

Commercial benefits such as agreements that contain tiered volume discounts to entice the customer to spend more with the supplier to gain the higher discount levels can be very effective.

Equally useful are extended warranty terms (guarantees), as discussed earlier in this book.

Usage-Based Charges

OEM after-sales can introduce "pay by the hour/usage" contracts where the customer pays a fixed amount for servicing based on the time the equipment is operating or in use. Customers value this format as it allows them to pay only their contracted fixed usage fee, irrespective of reliability. It effectively shifts the financial liability for product performance issues onto the supplier. Consequently, the supplier is motivated to manage and enhance reliability proactively to increase their profit margin. The knock-on effect for the customer is a better product and reduced operational disruption. This is another great example of adding value through servitization.

From the suppliers' perspective, if the customer sends the product elsewhere for MRO, they will still have to pay their contracted usage fee and the other providers' charges. This effectively means the customer would pay twice for the same service and so it creates exclusivity between the customer and the contracted supplier without an explicit reference.

As these agreements effectively deliver exclusivity by default, customers can view them with suspicion. Consequently, it is highly likely that price discounts and other incentives would also need to be included.

The after-sales team must weigh the pros and cons of binding customers to long-term deals for guaranteed cash flow, while also considering the risks of lower profit margins and exposure to variable reliability. OEMs typically prefer this type of agreement, as they have control over the design and financial risk of the product. But in recent years, even independent providers have offered similar types of deals.

IP Protection

The OEM can take much stronger control of their IP, including the monitoring of independent MRO stations and tracking who is purchasing their spares. This can allow them to either pursue revenue-generating licensing agreements or "cease and desist" action if they feel their IP is being abused.

Licensing arrangements can be attractive as while the supplier may offer a discount on spares and support, they might typically require the MRO provider to:

- Pay an annual license fee (which may or may not be sales volume related).
- Only use the OEM spares, which they purchase at standard lead time.
- Only use the OEM manuals.
- Purchase STTE as listed in the maintenance manuals, from the OEM.
- Restrict their usage of the IP provided by the OEM.

The reality is that no single action is going to be 100 percent successful in preventing competition. Instead, the problem needs to be addressed like spread betting; the more bases you can cover, the better your chances of winning. Therefore, view the items above as a set that showcases the actions that, when combined, will greatly enhance your business's preparedness and resilience against competitor attacks.

In summary, too many organizations are complacent about competition and the damage it can do. Countering proactively is simply more efficient than playing catch-up or trying to recapture what has been lost.

Top Tips

- Creating a central data repository and using standard KPIs as leading indicators will help detect competitive threats early. For example, simple but effective measures might include:
  - RFP/RFQ quantity trend.
  - RFP/RFQ win rate.
  - Contractual win rate.
  - Daily sales and orders versus forecast.
  - Level of general sales and customer service inquiries.
  - General market intel.

    Once again, an appropriate business system such as CRM is the ideal tool to manage and present these data.
- As discussed earlier, remember that a positive reaction to and management of competitors can also deliver beneficial outcomes for a business.
- Never lose sight of the simple fact that your business performance should always be the first line of defense against competition and, hence, the need for service excellence.

Marketing

Now that you have your product, completed business case, and primary value proposition ready (which may need some adjustments for each customer), the next step is marketing. Marketing is an essential element for the success of your business and is a subject extensively covered in published material. Hence, I will only focus on a few pertinent points from my career.

At its most basic, marketing is the process to ensure customers are both aware of your business and enticed to purchase your product/service offering. When implemented properly, it will secure the regular and effective distribution of your messages, ensuring your business remains a constant and relevant entity in the minds of your customers. However, many organizations still get the basics wrong, and the following represent just a few of the most common examples I have seen:

- Media such as flyers and brochures that look great but lack detail and so have no useful purpose for your customers.
- Expensive and complex websites/portals that lack useful customer content and/or are poorly maintained.
- Tradeshow booths that are just plain uninteresting. One example is using a cookie-cutter approach to design a product that matches competitors.
  - The practicality and visuals associated with the design are both critical; for example, one organization invested in a very expensive new booth, but tried to include every USP and value proposition written onto the vertical surfaces. What they produced were incredibly dull word walls that customers did not connect with.
- The invite list for expensive corporate events such as golf days, dinners, and so on, that includes "favorites" and "pals" but excludes key customer decision-makers.
- Regular events that have become burned into the calendar and so are "untouchable," although they produce little or no measurable benefit.

Many companies believe that pampering clients with extravagant hospitality leads to their happiness, despite consistently underperforming and disappointing those same customers. In fact, I have noticed that offering such levels of hospitality while failing to deal with performance issues just compounds the dissatisfaction. On multiple occasions, I have witnessed a CEO being skewered by a customer's straightforward question: "Why do you prioritize spending on entertainment over addressing the persistent performance issues you have?"

Looking back, although we can usually identify inappropriate marketing solutions, we also frequently witness the hijacking of good design and/or preparation. This is a phenomenon that is often observed when senior management, who are typically disconnected from the daily operations of customers and sales, insist on implementing their own solutions.

Unfortunately, I cannot offer any quick fix for the specific problem of meddlesome senior management. Trying to educate them to the error of their ways can certainly be difficult, and I have only one method that has consistently delivered any degree of success. This involves the use of unfavorable comparisons to your best-in-class competitors' offerings, for example, via a walking tour at a tradeshow. This can work, but it is not a guarantee of success, as sometimes leadership will have simply convinced themselves of their infallibility.

It is also necessary to briefly examine the importance of digital marketing and web portals to a business, its customers, and its market offering. In the past, a basic website was satisfactory. However, while they still hold considerable worth, portals have become increasingly significant in our personal and professional lives. As purchasing requirements have naturally evolved, organizations looking for a competitive edge have quickly adopted portals to offer something different.

So, why portals? Well, they can provide a focused point of entry to a controlled and potentially very broad spectrum of services and information. The "control" factor is important here as portals allow a business to restrict the audience permitted access to the information they are presenting. They can also allow the user to access information tailored to their specific business dealings with an organization.

In my experience, portals have always been beneficial, as they provide customers with easy access to critical information such as invoices, shipping data, technical documentation, promotions, and more.

Having a web portal in place can also be a very effective method of improving efficiency within your business, as introducing customer self-service and automation can significantly improve costs. Finally, a portal can also control the flow of IP, restricting access and ensuring traceability of who is accessing what.

A portal can also be part of an organization's value proposition, as the greater the benefit to the customer, the more value it carries. Nevertheless, it is crucial to exercise caution, as the absence of a user-friendly and beneficial portal can cause a detrimental outcome.

In truth, if you subject your customers to an inferior digital experience while your competitors provide superior ones, inevitably, you will lose both current and prospective clients. To highlight this, in a survey of 14,300 customers (mixed individual consumers and business buyers), 80 percent stated that the experience a company provides is as important as its products and services (Salesforce 2023).

Introducing portals can lead to more customer inquiries, especially during the initial phase of adjustment. Furthermore, it will set a higher level of expectation with your customers (making things simpler for them). Therefore, before you start any activity, there are some basic rules that many organizations fail to follow:

- Remember that the main purpose of a portal is to make life easier for your customers to interact with and learn about your business, so promptly addressing any user issues that arise is crucial. Consequently, you will need to ensure that your portal support team is prepared to expedite resolution of the many potential issues that your customers may have—for example, password and access problems, download issues, and general queries, and so on.
- Unlike websites, which typically contain static data, and generally entail a lower level of maintenance, by comparison, a portal will require more frequent day-to-day support. But whether you have a website or a portal, ensure that your team is prepared for the routine updates required to maintain relevance and value to your customers.
- A simple website may be entirely suitable for a business, so do not get carried away and believe that a portal is always a "must have." Instead, make sure that having a restricted user access area is appropriate and that your proposed content will be of interest and benefit to your existing and potential customers.

As I have stated many times in this book, nothing stands still; therefore, we must also be considering what comes next. For portals, you can now read *digital experience platforms (DXP)* as being the next evolution in digital marketing. DXPs extend far beyond portals, serving as the central hub for organizations to create, manage, and streamline customers' digital

journeys across their various channels seamlessly, even offering highly personalized experiences.

All the above points will need to be factored into your digital marketing assessment and planning. However, regardless of the challenges, having an appropriate digital interface, such as a website, portal, or DXP, can
be a powerful value creator and competitive differentiator for a business.

In summary, in terms of your day-to-day approach to marketing, best
practice is to utilize a multichannel approach, ensuring maximum reach.
For example, this might include printed industry-specific media, targeted
mailing campaigns (e-mail and/or snail mail), relevant social media, and
a strong digital interface (website/portal/DXP). But, regardless of your
choice, it is crucial to first create a marketing strategy that is tailored to
your business. Finally, make sure your products and services deliver customer satisfaction and target the appropriate audience. Otherwise, you
will waste considerable time and effort.

Top Tips

- Remember, it is a competitive world out there and so always
  do a sense check before proceeding with any marketing (and
  sales) projects. I would recommend deploying a "style council"
  composed of your best customer-facing employees and have
  them review all new material. If they do not believe that the
  proposed framing is correct and will lead to success, then you
  already have a sign that it probably will not be so. Not only
  will this save you considerable time and expense chasing the
  wrong ideas, it can also dramatically improve your success rate
  of those projects that proceed.
- Ensure that your marketing budget is being used effectively.
  This point may seem obvious, but many organizations overlook it as they focus on the spending, without monitoring
  their ROI. Therefore, make sure you have clear goals and set
  up KPIs that measure the results of each of your activities.
  Over time, this will ensure you can identify those areas of
  budget spend that deliver the most impactful results.

Conferences and Tradeshows

Another very effective way of marketing your business is without question via community gatherings such as tradeshows and conferences. These events gather many of your customers in one place, providing an efficient opportunity for you to engage with them in both business and social environments.

I have attended just about every type of customer gathering going, ranging from a simple small booth at a tradeshow, to customer feedback conferences and entertainment suites at international events. These are all equally effective forums to engage with your existing and potential customers. However, depending on the format, they can also be very challenging for you personally and for your business. For instance, customer/user forums can publicly expose all your product/service issues, so you will need to be well prepared for any potential negativity.

That said, user conferences can also be a great way to drive change within your organization. A good example might be with a particular design fault, or perhaps a pricing issue, where you are struggling to gain traction with a recalcitrant internal stakeholder. There will be times when a deadline hits, and you still have no workable solution. When that happens, I would recommend that you invite them to attend the next conference with you. Face-to-face pressure from customers is unparalleled in its ability to focus the mind, and there have been many occasions when such direct attention has caused these roadblocks to quickly dissolve.

I once had a thorny product performance issue that was creating high discontent among the customer base. We had already taken it to our design team following very negative feedback at the previous year's user conference. However, progress on a fix had been slow (well, static really).

With the next user conference approaching, we knew the company was going to be in a tough position. So, after some gentle nudging and encouragement, we managed to get a formal request from a key customer asking our engineering team to join us at the upcoming event and present their progress. We promptly forwarded the invitation to our Head of Engineering, informing them about the conference format, and the requirement for them to join the after-sales team on stage to represent the business. Subsequently, while the solution was not fully complete, it had progressed surprisingly rapidly, and the engineering team was able to deliver positive news at the conference.

They/we still did not escape without criticism and there was some proverbial "bruising" inflicted, but it was a lot calmer than it would have otherwise been. The Head of Engineering also had a good learning experience, as he had never experienced that type of "bear pit" forum before.

As a footnote, after this, we only had to mention the possibility of a user conference invite and our product design fixes gained significantly better resourcing and momentum. I cannot possibly think why!

There is a quick final point relating to tradeshow customer feedback that is worth mentioning. One often-repeated theme is that many such events and, by inference, the exhibitors, are "stuck in a routine." As a result, the shows lack imagination and can be tediously boring. I would guess that this is not the customer reaction you would be seeking. Indeed, if you are investing a significant amount of money in an expensive booth, exhibitor space, and staff travel and entertaining (T&E) costs, I am sure the last thing you want is to bore your customers.

If we assume that your aim is to excite and enthuse customers about your business, then potentially something needs to change. So, my simple advice is, do not be boring. There is no rule that you need to conform to the "usual," so do not be afraid to be different—be creative and challenge the norms.

Top Tips

- Allowing any customer complaint to score a "direct hit" (a complaint that you cannot respond to positively) in public will only encourage others to join in. As a result, customer forums can quickly degenerate into very bruising events. Therefore, in a typical "bear pit" style end-user conference, it is very important to manage the audience.

○ Prepare diligently and have a simple strategy to deal with the unexpected or "impossible to answer" questions, or just those agitated customers. Potential strategies could involve acknowledging the question and offering to schedule a side meeting to enable discussion of the response in greater detail.

By using this method, you can both positively respond and transition the conversation to a private setting. Importantly, it also creates space, allowing the customer to cool off.

○ Alternatively, if you are dealing with a vocal customer and the ringleader of complaints, try negotiating a solution directly with them before the event. This way, you can remove them and their influence from the situation.

• Just remember the mantra—"Do not allow a customer to draw blood in a public forum."

Mergers and Acquisitions

I would like to briefly talk about mergers and acquisitions (M&A), as this is another topic that introduces substantial change to organizations with varied results. Previous research has shown that between 70 and 90 percent of all M&A projects fail and that is a rather stark headline (Martin 2016, 4).

It is not unreasonable to expect that businesses making substantial investments in M&A activity would dedicate themselves to achieving success. Sadly, the reality is too many projects fail (to at least some degree). From what I have observed, while I agree that failure is prevalent, it is also important to consider the different levels of failure within the context of the statistics. Therefore, failure can range from a complete project failure to simply not meeting specific (but very important) measures of success.

Throughout the years, I have been directly impacted by or witnessed multiple M&A projects, and only one stands out as a success. For the other projects, the following points will highlight key areas where the

M&A implementation teams have failed to deliver. Sometimes, it may have been a few of these points, but, in unfortunate projects, it has been all of them.

Due Diligence

A lack of due diligence in the M&A discovery phase might seem like an oxymoron, but it surprisingly occurs. To undertake this task well, it requires having the people with the right knowledge and experience dedicated to the team. However, if an organization lacks dedicated M&A resources, day-to-day operational pressures may cause those best qualified to either be unavailable or simply unable to apply sufficient focus to the project.

Planning

A failure to define what post-merger success should be is not an uncommon occurrence. This point may be very simple, but without a clearly defined post-merger business vision, how can the implementation team prepare and deliver?

Measurement

Not creating and/or applying KPIs that measure the key success factors is also a regular oversight. In the absence of either clear metrics or a failure to measure, it becomes problematic to ascertain if the M&A is yielding the desired outcomes during or after the project.

Value

Failure to preserve the business value (the very reasons for the M&A) is a significant oversight. All too often, organizations pursue a business because it is "pink, shiny, and square-shaped," only to immediately turn it "brown, round, and fluffy"—so that it aligns with their existing business.

However well-intended those changes might have been, they can also be very effective value-destroyers. This can show up in different ways, but most often I have seen it as a clash of cultures and an inability to recognize the differences and address them proactively. For example, I have often noted the lead business will not investigate, recognize, and adopt best practices from the business they are acquiring and merging with. Cameron and Green (2015, 296) refer to this as "the way things are done around here." I have witnessed this, driven by the lead organization adopting a "not made here" superiority complex toward anything the other organization does. This is quite bizarre, given that many M&A projects are happening because the target business is good at what they do.

However, it is also worth noting that even when buying failed or substandard businesses, one can learn valuable lessons, even if it is just from their mistakes.

People

During the post-M&A integration activity, managers often adopt a tough approach toward the "subservient" organization's employees. Sometimes, this can seem like the Star Trek Borgs' belief that resistance is futile, and assimilation is a foregone conclusion!

I have seen the negative results of this manifest themselves in many ways, including "work to rule," "go-slows," unofficial overtime bans, and, at their worst, acts of sabotage. Not only can these actions be damaging to an organization's operations, but they can also directly lead to customer dissatisfaction, lost goodwill, and reduced sales.

Sometimes, it may be necessary to push through an M&A forcefully, especially with a failing business. However, it is still crucial to consider the morale and goodwill of the staff being retained.

Speed

Trying to drive a project to completion too quickly, without considering other factors, may yield short-term gains, but it can also impede the resolution of significant problems. Unfortunately, many times I have seen significant issues and negative KPIs being deliberately ignored to maintain the project timeline and avoid delays and complications.

Tick Box

Similar to the previous point, unfortunately, poorly deployed KPIs and financial incentivization for the project team can lead to undue pressure to either hit all the project steps and/or complete the project on time. This can mean the implementation team loses sight of the desired outcomes and instead adopts a tick-box mentality. The result of this can be very damaging to the project—even if they are aware of it.

Hidden Factory

Engineered products often have a *hidden factory* operating within the business. Failure to recognize this before M&A completion can have disastrous consequences for both operations and delivery. This is especially pertinent when planned low staff retention within the target organization compromises crucial knowledge transfer.

Negative employee reactions may also occur because of M&A activity. These might include an unexpected increase in staff turnover or a sudden shift to strictly following written instructions after project completion, disregarding previously developed informal operational efficiencies and solutions.

Rebranding

Driving the rebranding in an overly aggressive manner can also lead to loss of staff goodwill. Employees may have developed strong emotional connections with their organization, and so trying to eradicate all trace of that business with undue haste can create highly emotional (negative) responses.

Communication

I agree with Cameron and Green (2015, 272), who emphasize the importance of communication within the M&A activity. However, I would also assert that this applies equally to all stakeholders, including employees, customers, and investors.

Any lack of communication will create "gaps" in the M&A narrative that will always be filled with gossip and rumor. This can create additional anxiety and unhelpful outcomes. Therefore, it is critical to manage the communication process and content effectively. This should include conducting regular reviews, providing updates for all stakeholders, and promptly documenting and addressing any concerns or negative feedback.

Perhaps the main repetitive theme I have witnessed relates to the people and culture differences between businesses. I agree with Punit Renjen, Global CEO Emeritus of Deloitte:

> *For acquiring companies, the excitement is almost always about where they are going—that is, their strategy for gaining greater growth and productivity. But when mergers fail, it's often because no one focused on who they are—that is, their culture, which is critical to successfully bringing different groups of people together.*

In summary, I have seen any one and all the above negatively impact M&A. Therefore, I emphasize these issues deserve serious consideration, because they all possess the potential to destroy value, whether individually or together.

Top Tips

For anyone involved in M&A, a refresher on your schooldays physics might be helpful. Remember Newton's Third Law, "For every action, there's an equal and opposite reaction"? This principle also applies to M&A and on that basis, I strongly recommend a sense check on all decisions and actions before implementing them. It requires answering one simple question: Will the proposed action improve, maintain, or harm the target business's value? This one step of consciously evaluating the impact beforehand can prevent potentially very damaging actions.

CHAPTER 8

People Really Do Matter

Recruitment and Staff Retention

In 2019, *Harvard Business Review* published data from the U.S. Census and Bureau of Labor Statistics showing that 95 percent of hiring was undertaken to fill existing positions (Cappelli 2019, 4–5). While it may not be specific to the after-sales marketplace, it is at least indicative of a general issue.

High employee turnover is the enemy of organizations that rely on strong customer relationships and smooth-running functions to deliver optimal service and support. Managerial focus may divert from routine leadership duties toward recruitment, further disrupting established customer networks (Irons 1997, 169–170).

There is a famous quote attributed to Richard Branson of Virgin Atlantic fame "Clients do not come first. Employees come first. If you take care of your employees, they will take care of your customers." How true this is, and just how any business can expect disaffected or disenchanted employees to deliver great service levels to their customers, or even stay with the organization is a mystery to me.

Nobody comes into work intending to do a poor job or having an unpleasant experience. Instead, most employees want to enjoy their jobs, perform well, and receive reward/recognition for their efforts. In fact, employee relations equal customer relations—they are one and the same (Desatnick 1987, 15).

Having the right staff is always a challenge, regardless of whether you are a startup or an existing business. But whatever your situation, the same ground rules apply.

My advice for business success is to surround yourself with the best people possible, as no one person alone can make a business thrive (unless, of course, they are a sole trader). For clarity, that means you should look positively upon having people in your team who are already better than you or who have the capability to go further than you.

There is absolutely nothing wrong with being a trainer and producer of exceptional talent within a business, particularly if those staff who leave your team remain within the business. You can enjoy the benefits of having those great people while they are with you and watch as they grow and go on to greater things.

This approach is not completely selfless either. If you hire and train people for your business, they are likely to continue the values you have taught them, spreading likeminded individuals throughout your organization.

The after-sales team represents the external face of a business, so I always prioritize hiring individuals with exceptional communication skills. However, some of the other most important attributes I have found to be are out-of-the-box thinking, curiosity, problem-solving, resilience, strong customer focus, and a bias for action. These attributes are worth their weight in gold when the problems inevitably arrive, and, from bitter experience, I can confirm that when they do, it is invariably at the most inopportune moments.

In the past, the saying "all publicity is good publicity" may have held true. However, in today's marketplace, where social media has significant influence and customers are more sensitive, businesses should recognize adverse publicity as damaging to their reputation. To successfully address this, having customer-facing staff who deploy the key attributes I have just referred to is a prerequisite. Indeed, it is crucial to have staff members who do not accept the "computer says no" responses. Instead, they should take ownership of problems and drive innovative solutions that keep your business on track with your customers. These qualities will be critical to your sales and business longevity.

The top performers in the after-sales industry, through their actions and behavior, show a firm commitment to prioritizing customer needs and satisfaction. Of course, management can also deploy many additional motivators to ensure the right behaviors are being exhibited, such as incentive schemes and KPIs.

Having overseen the recruitment of many new employees, I am fully aware that, despite one's best efforts and thorough pre-employment screening, there will always be an element of the unknown. Therefore, recruitment always carries risk, and so the challenge is how you reduce that. Obviously, there are many companies offering to do this for you, although I must be honest and state that I have never resorted to that option. Instead, I have developed my strategy as follows:

1. The first hurdle to overcome is that too many organizations treat recruitment as an exclusive club, only allowing members (usually limited to HR, the hiring manager, and senior management) to take part. This approach and the reasons for allowing it to prevail have always bewildered me. I believe limits placed upon those entitled to be involved in the process are inversely proportional to the quality of the recruitment.

2. Next, my preferred approach is to use a simple layered candidate assessment process. Like my "style council" comments earlier in this book, this method would also include the experience and expertise of existing personnel from within the hiring organization.

3. The candidate assessment would begin with the usual panel-style interview. The panel would normally include at least one member of the current team from where the candidate would work and the hiring manager and an HR representative.

4. The candidate would then undergo a practical assessment tailored to the role being filled, that is, novice/trainee, or fully experienced. This might involve a written test, commentary on a subject, or a role-play with existing team members. You can choose to deliver this assessment either with or without warning, or you can send it to the candidate to prepare for or to complete in advance.

5. The closing element would be the typical walkaround facility tour, again conducted by members of the team where the candidate would work (greybeards are great for this). After completing the activity, each of the team members involved would complete standard scoring/feedback sheets, and the combined results would be used as part of the final selection.

Not only does this approach lead to better selection decisions, but having had the existing staff involved in the process provides for better acceptance and integration of the successful candidate.

I have never had a job applicant complain about this type of process, and many have responded positively. It is also interesting to note that the rigor of the process left those who were ultimately successful in being selected with significant feelings of pride and personal achievement.

In the current marketplace, you must also consider the future requirements and the growing trend of job candidates interviewing you as much as you interview them. Now, potential employees have new items on their wish list, such as gym memberships, onsite facilities, working from home (WFH), flexible hours, and mental health support. This list will continue to evolve as the job market changes. So, while money is still important, companies must now also consider many other factors.

Unsurpisingly, the best customer service businesses I have seen (and any other successful business for that matter) spend considerable effort seeking the very best new hires. Once employed, they treat their staff with respect, train them, motivate them, and recognize their efforts/accomplishments and reward them appropriately. This instills an organizational sense of purpose and belief in the direction of travel, and I would say these have always been and will continue to be the foundations of having and keeping outstanding employees.

According to Wilson et al. (2012, 257–258), the significance of attracting, developing, and retaining high-quality personnel within knowledge- and service-based sectors cannot be overstated. They also present a useful model for a business to deliver service quality through its employees based around four central themes. These are: (1) hire the right people, (2) develop people to deliver service quality, (3) provide the support systems needed, and (4) keep the best people. This is a very simple but effective strategy, and, while not using it specifically, I have certainly deployed its sentiments with considerable success.

In summary, the point I am trying to make, without going into excessive HR details, is that we need both great people and great support to build high-performance teams that deliver excellent service. Failure to do so risks wasting time and investment and can lead to revolving-door recruitment, negatively affecting both the customers and business results.

Top Tips

- Do not be afraid to experiment with the recruitment process you deploy. There is nothing wrong with testing and challenging candidates.
- Always seek feedback from each candidate for their views on the process—specifically asking how and where it can improve.

Team Management

For the purposes of this book, I am only going to focus on the structure of management decisions and how this relates to the team.

The first step is to decide the style of management you want (or maybe, are already delivering). Although many models/styles exist, I feel they can be simplified into two categories: autocratic and democratic.

Despite my extensive working career and many organizations and leaders that I have worked with, I have yet to see a truly best-in-class autocratically led business. But why is that the case?

I believe that the typical personality traits of the best after-sales teams do not align well with organizations where they have no say in decision-making. Maybe it is because no one likes to be blamed for the mistakes of others, and working in a heavily customer-focused market, an autocracy leaves you exposed in exactly that way. In addition, the attributes discussed in the previous chapter imply that after-sales personnel are independent thinkers and action-takers. Unfortunately, this can create conflicts in organizations where ideas and orders are strictly dictated from above. The leader's autocratic conduct may be perceived as disrespectful, predicated on the belief of their inherent superiority and the dismissal of employee input.

Personally, I am firmly in the "many hands make light work" school of thought, and, if I am working with great people, why would I not want their input?

I have found the best after-sales organizations are those that are based on democracy, actively encouraging input and debate. Once again, this aligns with the previously discussed "style council" approach. Incorporating current employees into the decision-making process offers many benefits, for example, the absence of consultancy costs. It also functions as a valuable strategy to combat "groupthink," stimulates employee interest by introducing challenges beyond their daily routine, and cultivates a sense of pride and involvement within the workforce.

The businesses that have embraced this approach have always emphasized the importance of teamwork, both within their own organization and in their interactions with customers. Their collaborative and inclusive approach further strengthens their team's foundation.

The only risk is that including everyone in every decision can be exhausting and slow down the process. Therefore, managing who contributes to the discussions is also crucial to ensure that only key/relevant stakeholders are involved.

However, reaching decisions via a truly democratic vote does not guarantee a problem-free solution either. I have seen this result in teams splitting into two or more opposing camps, each unable to accept the other's solution. From my experience, I have found that setting up key decisions as open discussions and involving the team in the leader's final decision is more productive.

In summary, the teams I have worked with accept the leader gets the final say on their inputs, and so I have always found this approach effective. Steve Jobs, cofounder, chairman, and CEO of Apple, emphasized this when he said, "Incredible things in the business world are never made by a single person, but by a team." Nobody would doubt that he was the driving force behind that organization, but he clearly credits the impact of the "team."

Based on my findings, I believe this is the best way to approach organizational decision-making—a hybrid method that involves collaboration and a final decision made by a leader after considering the options presented.

Top Tips

- Do not overlook the considerable benefits that can arise from leveraging your existing workforce and approaching their participation in decision-making with a constructive attitude.
- It is vital to carefully track the consequences of decisions and promptly modify, enhance, or replace them if negative outcomes occur, as enduring support hinges on positive results.

Training

"The only thing worse than training your employees and having them leave is not training them and having them stay,"

—Henry Ford, American industrialist
and business magnate.

I have observed throughout my career that many companies limit their training provision to introductory, on-the-job (OJT), and mandatory compliance needs such as health and safety, ethics, and anticorruption. Sadly, and as a result, many do not provide continuous role-specific vocational training to their employees. Despite this, I cannot remember a single instance where management has doubted the importance and value of vocational training. Regrettably, these positive feelings often do not result in any action.

For certain roles, OJT can of course be entirely sufficient on its own. However, for the critical customer-facing functions, a higher skill set is required to deliver service excellence.

I have forgotten the number of times I have heard a senior manager say, "But they are an experienced 'insert any role here' person and so they don't need training." Many times, they will not have even bothered to check whether that member of staff has ever had any specific formal training for their role.

From critical customer interface roles, your business will be demanding performance and results, whereas the customers expect courtesy, professionalism, and delivery. Working with customers day in and day out is undoubtedly high pressure and often very stressful, and I have proven that such roles always benefit from additional ongoing training.

It is imperative to have a team composed of the best professionals—those who consistently deliver outstanding results, demonstrate unwavering commitment, and have undergone comprehensive training in their respective fields. This is not only fundamental for achieving organizational success but also for their own personal development. So, I find it sad that any business would not provide initial and continuous vocational training to enable their personnel to excel in an ever-changing business landscape.

The following are just two examples of poor thinking related to training:

One organization I have experience with thought they were doing the right thing by essentially cancelling all vocational training for an extended period. The training budget was being used in what I refer to as "sheep dip mode" for reeducating all employees on a new business operating system.

Unfortunately for them, the project was both poorly thought through and just some questions that arose were:

- Why did every member of staff need to go through the same training?
- If all employees required training for the new business operating system, why was it not budgeted for separately?
- If everyone agreed specific staff needed vocational training to perform their jobs, why did they cancel it, given the obvious implications for suboptimal ongoing performance?

The outcomes were made worse because the new business operating system had only a very limited impact on the organization's performance after 12 months. Yet, despite this being widespread knowledge, training restrictions persisted in the business. The result was a noticeable loss of confidence in the new system and senior management, which was far from ideal.

The second and very simple example relates to an organization that wanted to improve the effectiveness of their sales function. Having identified knowledge gaps, the sales team promptly chose an appropriate external course. Management subsequently rejected the course (too expensive). Then, management assigned HR the task of finding a more "suitable" (cheaper) course, which they accomplished, and the sales team attended. However, the focus on price meant HR had neglected to conduct thorough due diligence. As a result, they had neither adequately mapped the training needs of those involved nor accurately assessed the training outcomes sought by the business against the course content.

The result—well, the sales team enjoyed a few days away on full expenses in a pleasant hotel but learned very little of benefit. Likewise, the business came away with an underwhelming ROI and had to redo the training later. Therefore, poor planning required the business to pay twice for the training. They also faced the added penalty of having staff missing from the business for extra days and performing at a lower level for an extended period.

These examples (aside from the questionable impact of the new business system) demonstrate a failure to adequately plan by not ensuring full alignment of training needs, outcomes, and course content.

Therefore, my clarion call to all businesses is—training is an absolute fundamental enabler to delivering after-sales excellence and so ensure that you are creating and delivering appropriate vocational training plans.

Top Tips

- Formal, lengthy, and expensive training should not be a prerequisite. I have utilised experienced individuals within a business, and myself, to deliver both formal and informal training. Besides the obvious benefits of knowledge transfer within a business, assigning training responsibilities and targets to existing team members can also recognize their abilities and offer them rewarding challenges.
- When organizing functional training, ensure that all the team members attend, including the greybeards. Those in the latter group often push back, arguing that the training is beneath them. However, I have found that when everyone on the team attends, it significantly enhances team spirit.
- The contributions of senior staff during any tuition can be highly valuable. They can provide support for and context to a tutor's material, especially if the latter is external and unfamiliar with the business. To secure the support of these team members, highlight the significance of their knowledge and

roles as "assistant tutors." If nothing else, this is an effective way to appeal to their vanity.
- With the greybeards, I also firmly believe that it is never too late to teach an old dog new tricks or remind them of poor habits they may have fallen into.

Managing Change

Everything that has preceded this chapter so far sets up the potential for amendment, alteration, new processes, new systems, training, and so on, and, at every level, that means change, both large and small. Hence, I would be negligent if I did not mention the subject of change management, especially because if you execute it well, it will support your journey toward achieving after-sales excellence.

First, it is worth simply emphasizing that change is good, and it is necessary. In the words of former U.S. President John F. Kennedy, "Change is the law of life and those who look only to the past or present are certain to miss the future." I have repeatedly talked about the fluidity of the after-sales marketplace, and, therefore, if you are still running your business the same way as you did 5 to 10 years ago, alarm bells should be ringing.

No customer or market remains unchanged, and, if we acknowledge the necessity of a response to that from our organizations, the effectiveness of managing that process becomes crucial. Given that operating landscape, it is perhaps surprising to highlight that failure is commonplace, with research showing that only approximately 31 percent of change management projects are successful (Nieto-Rodriguez 2023, 2). You might wonder what could cause such a low success rate and, based on my observations, the following play a major part:

- Failure to understand the organization's capability and capacity to accept and deliver change.
- Rushed and/or poor planning.
- Failure to deploy in line with the plan.
- Inadequate definition of the post-project deliverables and expectations.

- Missing KPIs enabling effective monitoring of both project progression and post-project results.
- Poor communication.
- Lack of staff (and other stakeholder) engagement.

While all the factors mentioned above have contributed to negative results, I have found the most common significant causes of change project failure to be a lack of organizational preparedness, poor communication, and engagement.

A business I worked with had a major new ERP system rollout planned for its after-sales division. It launched the project and began assigning the existing process experts and greybeards from within the workforce to the project team on a part-time basis.

Many of the staff members assigned were long-serving employees with very limited experience of modern ERP systems, and yet, no additional training requirements were identified or deployed. As the project progressed and it became clear that the timelines were at risk, those same staff were then assigned full time to the project. Concurrently, the organization did not provide additional resources to those employees left managing daily operations, yet expected them to maintain the organization's financial and operational targets.

Incidentally, none of business targets either reflected or provided any leeway for the loss of resources to the project or the potential business disruption from the ERP rollout. This meant a significantly increased workload, level of expectation, and stress on all the affected staff.

When the project reached its target launch date, many of the critical go/no-go stage gates were still red (or incomplete). Despite these factors, the executives went ahead with the launch.

What happened? Well, unsurprisingly, the rollout was not an initial success, and it took many months before the organization returned to something even approaching stable business operations. The workforce experienced much higher levels of stress, and there were significantly higher levels of dissatisfied customers during this period.

Furthermore, although project team leaders received substantial bonuses for timely project completion, other employees—both project participants and those maintaining the ongoing business operations—received no bonus because of unmet routine business financial and operational KPIs.

The outcome of this was a seriously disaffected workforce and an ongoing malaise throughout the business for many months after.

Perhaps you can recall my earlier comments about badly designed KPIs and the law of unintended consequences, and this is another obvious example of exactly that in operation.

For a business to place its employees in a position where they can only fail because of its own inadequacies is both unfair and unacceptable. It will not deliver the required results and, worse still, will result in a loss of trust and motivation, employee resignations, and, worst of all, degraded business performance and reputational damage.

Before you start any project, it is vital to take stock of your organization's experience, capabilities, and capacity for change. This must be a rational review of the expectations for both the project and the ongoing business deliverables, timelines, and resourcing. Taking a balanced and fair-minded approach to these challenges will be vital to gaining your employees' support, and that will be critical to ensuring successful outcomes.

The general reality of any change, and no matter how positive the outcomes are, your employees will sit somewhere on a sliding scale of resistance. Depending on their own and the organizations' experience of change, their responses are likely to range anywhere between curious but unsure, to downright opposed. Regarding the latter, this can manifest itself with staff being unhelpful, or their performance drops, or they resign either during or post-project completion. Those who choose to leave the organization effectively resolve the problem. However, it is necessary to proactively manage the situation for those who stay and display negative performance or behavior, as their impact on others during and after can be corrosive if not addressed.

Remember to consider your other stakeholders: customers, suppliers, and investors. It is very poor practice to implement transformational, or indeed any changes that have implications for their relationships with you, with no warning. Keeping this group of interested parties regularly updated about both your intentions (pre-project launch) and progress during deployment gives them the opportunity to present their concerns and questions related to your plan. This way, you can keep all the relevant stakeholders engaged, informed, and, hopefully, confident about the outcomes.

In a previous chapter, I discussed the challenges associated with autocratic organizations, and those same challenges also apply here. Change should always be inclusive, but that is not always the case. Based on my involvement with many change projects, I do not believe that any employee likes change being "done to them." Enabling them to contribute their expertise on processes, potential challenges, and have direct input to the planning and deployment is essential for both their engagement and the realization of successful results. Without this employee participation, any change is likely to be regarded with suspicion (Bell and Patterson 2007, 162).

I have also noticed that selecting project team members strategically, even including those who may be openly resistant, can help maintain smooth progress in two ways. First, once integrally involved in a project, it becomes significantly more difficult for those opponents to maintain their previous negative position. Second, having those with strident negative views directly involved can send a clear visual message to any remaining opponents that the change is going ahead and maybe they should not fear it.

Throughout my career, I have always presented change as having positive outcomes for those involved. By consistently focusing on making sure the projects enhance the team's job satisfaction and efficiency, it has been much easier to secure their support. It is important to note that these projects have not solely focused on internal matters. By also improving external communication, delivery, and customer support, the team can effectively reduce complaints and minimize waste and resulting stress.

Trust is crucial for engaging in change. The employees need to have trust in the change process, which relies on effective communication, support, and successful outcomes. One of the key challenges for me was to shift the narrative from fear, concern, and stress to excitement, adventure, and anticipation of better times. So, for example, if you are working with a new team, try some smaller quick-win projects first. This helps to establish credibility and can kick-start the desire for more.

I covered an excellent example of this approach earlier in the "Customer Service" chapter. There, we had a large project that was going to be quite radical for a business that had experienced minimal change over an extended period. So, we took the full project and broke it down into smaller sections ("changelets"). By doing so, it was less daunting for the team—they got to see quick incremental wins, and so their confidence and engagement grew.

As a matter of fact, embedding a quick-win approach has additional advantages. The positive results encourage employees to take the initiative in identifying new opportunities to deliver improvement. They also help to develop an increasingly nimble organization to deal with both the ever-changing business environment and customer expectations (Bell and Patterson 2007, 168).

Determining the value of change projects can be challenging. Therefore, test projects to assess customer benefits before investing. By prioritizing customer outcomes in decision-making, you avoid getting involved in projects that may disappoint. When an organization sees positive outcomes and embraces change, it gains momentum and a desire for more. This is a healthy development.

In summary, in today's rapidly evolving marketplace, it is vital that each business has an ongoing change process, ensuring that your business is prepared for what tomorrow brings.

Top Tips

- Some businesses operate to a program of larger changes with a significant elapsed time between each. Although this may be appropriate at times, it can also be highly disruptive for both the staff and the business in general, as substantial changes equal large disturbance. Furthermore, by adopting this approach, performance will experience larger swings. This happens because many change requirements are "parked" awaiting the next major change event, instead of being implemented when they are initially needed.

Therefore, what I have learned is that making regular small changes and improvements not only minimizes disruption but also leads to the earlier achievement of the business performance being sought.

- If there is the bandwidth within your organization, consider having your change projects managed by a single team/individuals. This way you can ensure consistency of approach and continually build deployment expertise based on the experience gained from each project completed.

- Every completed change project presents an opportunity to improve your organization's knowledge via "lessons learned." Hence, it is vital to always complete a post-project analysis that incorporates both an evaluation of the actual results versus the planned objectives and reviews the positives and negatives that were seen during the process.

CHAPTER 9

Final Thoughts

I have seen much that is good, bad, and questionable with after-sales delivery throughout my 46 years of business service and, unsurprisingly, a lot of everything between. But I have thoroughly enjoyed every moment, and I am very fortunate that my career has given me an unusually broad and deep understanding of both bad and good practice.

Considering my prior comments, you might assume I oppose OEMs; however, this is simply not accurate. My stance is simply one that opposes anything that hampers business returns or results in subpar customer service, which are essentially the same.

I make no apologies for repeating the quotation presented much earlier in this book, "Most companies either don't know how or don't care to provide after-sales services effectively. Top managements the world over treat aftermarket services as a mere afterthought" (Cohen et al. 2006, 1). However, this is not limited to OEMs, as my career observations confirm many independent organizations similarly underachieve.

My experience has also repeatedly shown that an organization can reap significant benefits by implementing basic good practice and well-established improvement methods and striving for after-sales excellence. These benefits include:

- Simplicity and efficiency of operation.
- Protection of IP.
- Cost reduction.
- A strong pipeline of sales opportunities.
- Revenue and profit growth optimization.
- Resilience to external competition.
- Business longevity.
- Improved customer loyalty and satisfaction.
- Happy employees and low staff turnover.

Throughout this book, I have also consistently underscored the significance of cultivating effective relationships and collaborations between you, your business, and others. The understanding and management of relationships with employees, colleagues, peers, customers, and competitors will play a crucial role in determining your success. So, listen to them intently and manage your business relationships professionally, as people really do matter.

Clearly, how after-sales operates presents significant challenges and that will not ease. Ultimately, it all boils down to "serve, satisfy, repeat," and the landscape within which that activity is undertaken is constantly changing.

The enemy of change is complacency—it is one of the most pernicious elements to infiltrate and undermine business performance. It can negatively impact the performance in any area of an organization—from the management of customers and competitors, to processes and systems and everything between. Therefore, standing still is not an option; instead, every business should be on the front foot, constantly reacting to the changes in their surrounding landscape.

I am not brave enough to suggest that there is a "one-size-fits-all" solution to be followed. Therefore, to identify the right answer for your business, it is crucial to maintain flexibility, adaptability, and stay up to date about your specific market.

The size of the challenge (mountain or molehill) will, of course, be different for everyone, but I trust you can see the benefits of proactively deploying improvement and change. Regardless of the scale, now is the ideal time to embark on the after-sales excellence journey.

It would be fair to say that, unless you have had experience of managing change, it can seem a little overwhelming at the beginning. I would certainly be very cautious about starting with a large-scale project; yes, they remain important but temper your enthusiasm. Adopting a "go large" strategy is commendable, but it will have a longer gestation period, greater complexity, and be significantly more disruptive in delivery.

So, rather than trying to eat the entire cake at once, I would strongly recommend focusing on delivering smaller projects well. Adopting such an approach can deliver quick incremental gains. Additionally, when you achieve positive outcomes, you will gain valuable experience and generate organizational enthusiasm for more change, thus enabling the proverbial "snowball rolling downhill" effect.

Finally, getting any project launched requires overcoming inertia. However, as the saying goes, "practice makes perfect" and so just pick something appropriate and get started.

It is time to take a step back and review the broader perspective again. It is extremely important that you do not lose sight of the simple fact that despite all the disappointments, frustrations, and barriers, you need customers and (hopefully) they need you. Therefore, common ground already exists, and so you are potentially already two steps ahead.

How do you make it work from there onwards? Perhaps one of the most important points I will make is that delivering great after-sales service is generally not rocket science—at least not when you consider most of the issues covered in this book. The content largely presents uncomplicated material, but these are the most frequently occurring difficulties I have seen undermining organizations throughout my career. Therein lies both the bad and the good. The bad news is that many organizations and individuals get these basics wrong. The good news is that with some simple guidance and a willingness to embrace positive change, significant improvement is often well within reach.

We are all customers at some point, and so we already possess a sound idea of what is good and bad. If you can tap into that basic knowledge with common sense, determination, and purpose, you can build firm foundations for any business. Nothing inspires confidence more than seeing or experiencing something accomplished professionally. Thereafter, keeping and growing what you already have and adding fresh growth will be the ongoing challenges for your organization.

In writing this book, my utmost hope is that it provides valuable insights and solutions for business professionals, organizations and students, propelling their after-sales business knowledge and performance to the next level. If that happens, then it will prove to me that this venture into book writing has been a worthwhile exercise.

After-sales is a cornerstone of sustainability and profitability, extending product life, reducing waste, conserving resources, and cutting emissions. By keeping products in use through repairs, upgrades, and refurbishment, it reduces the need for resource-intensive manufacturing. In today's economic and environmental climate, after-sales is not optional—it is the engine of loyalty, profit, and long-term brand strength.

Finally, I have been considering how to sign off, and so here goes.

If you want to deliver outstanding results through after-sales and service excellence and aim to have a business that can be regarded as a benchmark in your market, then the following summarizes the advice:

> *Set your business ethos to one that expects ongoing review, challenge, and change. Watch your competitors closely and always know exactly what your customers want today and tomorrow, then deliver it well and at a fair price.*

If that can be the mantra of your business, you will not go too far wrong.

About the Author

Nigel Woodall is a married UK resident with two adult children and lives in the south of England.

My professional journey began in 1979 as an engineering apprentice with a UK airline. Subsequently, I progressed through various management and senior leadership positions within SMEs and multinational corporations, encompassing airlines, OEMs, and independent maintenance and spares distribution providers. These have all been business-to-business (B2B) roles and have included all the customer-facing functions, for example, sales and marketing, customer service, account management, product and technical support, commercial/contracts, and, finally, spares and repair services management.

I gained an MBA in 2005 and, over the years, have also been a speaker at many industry events and conferences. This experience has provided me with an unusually broad and deep understanding of the after-sales marketplace.

Throughout my career, I have always enjoyed tackling challenges and delivering organizational improvement, be that at a strategy, process, or people level, but the COVID-19 crisis prompted some valuable self-reflection. The result was that rather than heading back out to the "employee" workspace again, I set up my own business to share some of the valuable lessons that I have learned during my career. Since then, I have independently operated a successful post-sales business management consultancy, advising companies on enhancing customer-facing aspects of their after-sales operations to deliver optimum ROI. This focus on delivering maximum stakeholder benefit through enhanced service has been a key focus of much my career.

In late 2023, following discussion with and encouragement from clients and colleagues, I began writing this manuscript—my first venture into book authorship. It has since become both a hobby and labor of love, and I hope you enjoy it and benefit from the guidance it offers.

Having taken the time to read my book (thank you), I would be very grateful if you could also leave an online review.

References

Bell, Chip R., and John R. Patterson. 2007. *Customer Loyalty Guaranteed: Create, Lead, and Sustain Remarkable Customer Service.* Adams Business.

Boegershausen, Johannes, Noah Castelo, Christian Hildebrand, and Alexander P. Henkel. 2023. "Creating Customer Service Bots That People Don't Hate." *Harvard Business Review,* October. https://hbr.org/2023/10/creating-customer-service-bots-that-people-dont-hate.

Brandenburger, Adam, and Barry Nalebuff. 2021. "The Rules of Co-opetition." *Harvard Business Review,* January–February. https://hbr.org/2021/01/the-rules-of-co-opetition.

Buell, Ryan W. 2018. "The Parts of Customer Service That Should Never Be Automated." *Harvard Business Review,* February. https://hbr.org/2018/02/the-parts-of-customer-service-that-should-never-be-automated.

The Business Research Company. 2024. "Coffee Capsule Global Market Report 2024." https://www.thebusinessresearchcompany.com/report/coffee-capsule-global-market-report.

Buttle, Francis, and Stan Maklan. 2015. *Customer Relationship Management. Concepts and Technologies.* 3rd ed. Routledge.

Cameron, Esther, and Mike Green. 2015. *Making Sense of Change Management.* Kogan Page.

Cappelli, Peter. 2019. "Your Approach to Hiring Is All Wrong." *Harvard Business Review,* May–June. https://hbr.org/2019/05/your-approach-to-hiring-is-all-wrong.

CarTakeBack. 2023. "UK Scrap Cars." https://www.cartakeback.com/uk-scrap-cars/.

CB Insights, cited Fortune. 2014. "Why Startups Fail, According to Their Founders." https://fortune.com/2014/09/25/why-startups-fail-according-to-their-founders/.

Clutterbuck, David, Graham Clark, and Colin Armistead. 1993. *Inspired Customer Service. Strategies for Service Quality.* Kogan Page Limited.

Cohen, M. A., N. Agrawal, and V. Agrawal. 2006. "Winning in the Aftermarket." *Harvard Business Review.* https://hbr.org/2006/05/winning-in-the-aftermarket.

Daugherty, Paul R., H. James Wilson, and Karthik Narain. 2023. "Generative AI Will Enhance—Not Erase Customer Service Jobs." *Harvard Business Review,*

March. https://hbr.org/2023/03/generative-ai-will-enhance-not-erase-customer-service-jobs

Deloitte. 2020. "After-Sales Services. Transforming Manufacturing in the Wake of the COVID-19 Pandemic." https://www2.deloitte.com/us/en/insights/industry/manufacturing/aftermarket-services-digital-differentiator-beyond-COVID-19.html.

Desatnick, Robert L. 1987. *Managing to Keep the Customer. How to Achieve and Maintain Superior Customer Service Throughout the Organization*. Jossey Bass Inc.

Gallo, Amy. 2014. "The Value of Keeping the Right Customers." *Harvard Business Review*, October. https://hbr.org/2014/10/the-value-of-keeping-the-right-customers

Grandey, Alicia, A., and Kayley Morris. 2023. "Robots Are Changing the Face of Customer Service." *Harvard Business Review*, March. https://hbr.org/2023/03/robots-are-changing-the-face-of-customer-service.

Hart, Christopher W., James L. Heskett, and W. Earl Jr. Sasser. 1990. "The Profitable Art of Service Recovery." *Harvard Business Review*, July–August. https://hbr.org/1990/07/the-profitable-art-of-service-recovery.

Heppell, Michael. 2015. *5 Star Service. How to Deliver Exceptional Customer Service*. Pearson Education Limited.

Hughes, Jonathan, and Danny Ertel. 2020. "What's Your Negotiation Strategy?" *Harvard Business Review*, July–August. https://hbr.org/2020/07/whats-your-negotiation-strategy.

Irons, Ken. 1997. *The World of Superservice. Creating Profit Through a Passion for Customer Service*. Addison Wesley Longman Limited.

Jobber, David, and Geoff Lancaster. 2009. *Selling and Sales Marketing*. Pearson Education Limited.

Kannan, P. V., and Josh Bernoff. 2019. "Does Your Company Really Need a Chatbot?" *Harvard Business Review*, May. https://hbr.org/2019/05/does-your-company-really-need-a-chatbot.

Kaplan, Robert S., and David P. Norton. 1996. *The Balanced Scorecard. Translating Strategy into Action*. Harvard Business School Press.

Karsaklian, Eliane. 2019. *The After-Deal. What Happens After You Close a Deal?* Information Age Publishing, Inc.

Markey, Rob. 2020. "Are You Undervaluing Your Customers?" *Harvard Business Review*, January–February. https://hbr.org/2020/01/are-you-undervaluing-your-customers.

Martin, Roger L. 2016. "M&A: The One Thing You Need to Get Right." *Harvard Business Review*. https://hbr.org/2016/06/ma-the-one-thing-you-need-to-get-right.

Mayer, David, and Herbert M. Greenberg. 2006. "What Makes a Good Salesman." *Harvard Business Review*, July–August. https://hbr.org/2006/07/what-makes-a-good-salesman.

Nieto-Rodriguez, Antonio. 2023. "Organize Your Change Initiative Around Purpose and Benefits." *Harvard Business Review*, May. https://hbr.org/2023/05/organize-your-change-initiative-around-purpose-and-benefits.

Oliver Wyman. 2023. "Global Fleet and MRO Market Forecast 2023–2033." https://www.oliverwyman.com/our-expertise/insights/2023/feb/global-fleet-and-mro-market-forecast-2023-2033.html.

Palmer, Adrian. 2010. *Principles of Services Marketing*. McGraw-Hill Education.

Porter, Michael E. 2004. *Competitive Advantage*. Free Press.

Qualtrics XM Institute. 2024. "$3.7 Trillion of 2024 Global Sales are at Risk Due to Bad Customer Experiences." https://www.xminstitute.com/blog/trillion-sales-at-risk-2024/

Ryals, Lynette. 2012. "How to Succeed at Key Account Management." *Harvard Business Review*, July. https://hbr.org/2012/07/how-to-succeed-at-key-account?autocomplete=true.

Saffo, Paul. 2007. "Six Rules for Effective Forecasting." *Harvard Business Review*, July–August. https://hbr.org/2007/07/six-rules-for-effective-forecasting.

Salesforce. 2023. "State of the Connected Customer Report. 6th Edition." https://www.salesforce.com/uk/resources/research-reports/state-of-the-connected-customer/?cta-bottom-row-1-state_of_connected_customer.

Semler, Ricardo. 1999. *Maverick. The Success Story Behind the World's Most Unusual Workplace*. Random House Group Limited.

Smith, Ross, Mayte Cubino, and Emily McKeon. 2025. *The AI Revolution in Customer Service and Support*. Pearson Education Inc.

Statista. 2023. "Size of the global automotive after-sales 2016–2025." https://www.statista.com/statistics/581758/size-of-global-automotive-parts-aftermarket/.

Statista. 2024. "Average Age of Airplanes Removed from the Global Aircraft Fleet from 2005 to 2019, by Aircraft Type (in Years)." https://www.statista.com/statistics/622600/average-age-of-jets-when-removed-from-service-by-type/.

UK Customer Service Institute. 2025. "UK Customer Satisfaction Index (UKCSI)." https://www.instituteofcustomerservice.com/raising-customer-satisfaction/

U.S. Bureau of Labor Statistics. 2024. "Ted: The Economics Daily: 34.7 Percent of Business Establishments Born in 2013 Were Still Operating in 2023." https://www.bls.gov/opub/ted/2024/34-7-percent-of-business-establishments-born-in-2013-were-still-operating-in-2023.htm.

Walker, Scott. 2024. "Negotiate Like a Pro." *Harvard Business Review*, March–April. https://hbr.org/2024/03/negotiate-like-a-pro.

Wilson, Alan, Valarie A. Zeithaml, Mary Jo Bitner, and Dwayne D. Gremler. 2012. *Services Marketing. Integrating Customer Focus Across the Firm.* McGraw-Hill Education.

World Bank Group. 2025. "GDP (current US$)." https://data.worldbank.org/indicator/NY.GDP.MKTP.CD

Zeithaml, Valarie A., A. Parasuraman, and Leonard L. Berry. 1990. *Delivering Quality Service. Balancing Customer Perceptions and Expectations.* The Free Press.

Contact/Follow Up

In business, there is no doubt that the adage "nobody is perfect" applies. The reasons for this are many and varied, encompassing complacency, inadequate oversight, inexperience, excessive workloads, and a multitude of other possibilities.

Although internal solutions are possible for some organizations, an external, impartial perspective devoid of political or historical obligations to an organization can prove to be a highly effective strategy for many others.

However, as I have stressed many times already, the factors critical to success—good planning and due diligence—equally apply before selecting an external consultant.

My top tip for this process is to look for an organization that will **guide and assist your** business to both identify the "problem" and deliver the change. Therefore, your chosen partner should be one that will freely share their knowledge with you. Only that way will your organization gain the required understanding of the best approach and methods and build a level of self-sufficiency. A failure to acknowledge this very important point can lead to an ongoing reliance on external consultants, and that can become a very expensive habit.

If you would like to learn more about the issues raised in this book and/or about my consultancy business, then please get in touch via my website:

Website: www.aftermarketadvisoryconsulting.org

Index

www.ingramcontent.com/pod-product-compliance
Lightning Source LLC
Chambersburg PA
CBHW061200220326
41599CB00025B/4545